Praise for *Miss Memory Lane*

"Colton Haynes's memoir is as provocative as it is moving. In searing, honest prose, he tells a coming-of-age story that is utterly his own, yet surprisingly universal."

—Bill Clegg, *New York Times* bestselling author of
Portrait of an Addict as a Young Man

"*Miss Memory Lane* is a brutally honest memoir that socks you in the gut with its candor. Colton Haynes is a true survivor and shows us how conquering our demons in life is a never-ending journey."

—Elton John and David Furnish

"By confronting his own past, Colton Haynes challenges us to reflect upon the brutality seething just under the surface of the Hollywood dream."

—Saeed Jones, author of *How We Fight for Our Lives*

"Pairing vulnerability with unflinching prose, actor Haynes debuts with a deeply affecting look at his path to self-acceptance. . . . Fans will be left breathless by the grit and courage on display."

—*Publishers Weekly*

"Haynes's moving, open-hearted, courageous memoir is a complex story of familial losses and the loss of innocence, but it is nevertheless written with great simplicity. Readers will find it hard to resist."

—*Library Journal* (starred review)

"A vulnerable meditation on gender, desire, and fame, compelling and nuanced, a sensitive self-portrait woven from fragments of his past."

—BuzzFeed

"Impossible to put down . . . This is a gripping memoir, and what shines through is Haynes's clear-eyed wish to be honest with himself and with his readers about his actions."

—*Amazon Book Review*

MISS MEMORY LANE

a Memoir

COLTON HAYNES

ATRIA PAPERBACK

NEW YORK LONDON TORONTO SYDNEY NEW DELHI

ATRIA
PAPERBACK

An Imprint of Simon & Schuster, Inc.
1230 Avenue of the Americas
New York, NY 10020

First Atria Paperback edition March 2023

ATRIA PAPERBACK and colophon are trademarks of
Simon & Schuster, Inc.

For information about special discounts for bulk purchases,
please contact Simon & Schuster Special Sales at 1-866-506-1949 or
business@simonandschuster.com.

The Simon & Schuster Speakers Bureau can bring authors to your live event.
For more information or to book an event, contact the Simon & Schuster
Speakers Bureau at 1-866-248-3049 or visit our website at
www.simonspeakers.com.

Interior design by Erika R. Genova

Manufactured in the United States of America

1 3 5 7 9 10 8 6 4 2

Library of Congress Cataloging-in-Publication Data has been applied for.

ISBN 978-1-9821-7617-4
ISBN 978-1-9821-7618-1 (pbk)
ISBN 978-1-9821-7619-8 (ebook)

To all the queer kids who long for love and attention,
to the ones who'd break their own arm,
if only to have somebody sign their cast . . .
know that you are deserving of love without pain.

And to my beautiful mother,
I look for you in every smoke signal I send,
in every glance in the rearview, down every road I travel.
I will always love you.

PROLOGUE

First, there is a road, a road that takes me away from my house in the San Fernando Valley, the house where I live alone with the picture of a buffalo my mother sketched in pencil on a white canvas hanging above the fireplace. That road takes me east of there and south, past the shake shop on Hollywood Boulevard where I would sit and eat fries and drink a chocolate malt and study the black-and-white faces of the old movie stars plastered on the walls. Just south of there is Cherokee Park, where my mother told me she did drugs for the first time when she was a seventeen-year-old runaway and a bad shot made her wrist blow up like a balloon. A little bit west of there is the convenience store where I bought my first legal beer, twenty-one and on a tear, and a few blocks farther is the tower on Sunset where I saw my face on the side of a building for the first time, my chin tilted toward the camera and my eyes looking down, all of me plastered twenty stories high and gazing out over the city. I keep driving. There's a trance beat playing from the stereo, cigarette ash on the dashboard, crushed fast-food bags on the passenger side, a banana peel on the back seat like an unfinished joke. I let the beat drive me as the buildings whip past.

In the trunk of my car are shoeboxes and duffel bags and plastic containers stuffed to the brim with photographs and notebooks and letters, everything I could find about who I'd been. I spent all night combing through pictures, reading old diaries, searching long-abandoned email accounts. I do this most nights. I'm trying to find something in my past—the way a detective in the movies might search when they're just about to crack the case—a bloodhound sniffing the air, evidence tacked to a corkboard with pushpins that you study, waiting for the shape to reveal itself. To anyone else, all those pieces of myself I shoved into my car would look like a bunch of old junk. To me they are clues, a scavenger hunt with an unknowable prize, mile markers that, if followed correctly, will lead me somewhere important. I keep driving. East and out of the city, on the widening freeway, past strip malls and drive-thrus, pawn shops and liquor stores, that same beat playing, frenetic as my heart. Red and blue flashing lights in the rearview, but not for me, and for an instant I can remember the heavy weight of a police badge I once held in my teenage hand, the metallic chill of a gun. When I pass the exit for Hemet, I can smell my mother's perfume.

The road—it takes me farther into the desert, past the fields of wind turbines outside Palm Springs, past the hotel where I kissed my husband's face in front of a hundred guests, past the facility where I was wheeled in for twenty-eight days, wearing Jackie O sunglasses, and still I drive, faster now, pumping the accelerator under my foot, willing the car to fly. There were so many roads, and when I look back at them, I can visualize it all like a map: a path cut through the sun-bleached Kansas fields, Canal Street teeming with activity, a trail that led from a white-sand beach on the Florida Panhandle back to the highway, and this—this road, the one that I am on now, taking me away from where I was. I tell myself that this is my one last trip down memory lane.

I don't know where I'm going, but I am beginning to see where I've been.

PART
ONE

1

HOT SPRINGS, ARKANSAS
1992

I was four, and we were in Hot Springs, Arkansas, a town where the debutantes dined on chicken-fried steak at the Arlington Hotel, a town where it was better to be seen than heard, and I would have just about died for somebody to pay attention to me. I would have set the Arlington Hotel on fire if I'd thought it would make my mom turn to me and smile.

But I never would have done that, because my mom and I both loved the Arlington Hotel more than anywhere else in the world. It towered over a wide green lawn like a castle from Candyland, a proud American flag whipping in the wind above the tall stone steps leading up to the ornate entrance. Inside, past a grand piano, you followed the black-and-white-checkered linoleum tiles, gripping tightly onto the black banister that spiraled two times down to the basement, which led to a video arcade that was always empty, the Galaga and Pac-Man boxes lit up like Christmas trees, and a machine containing brightly colored spheres of bubble gum the size of golf balls you could buy for a quarter. My mom knew a secret trick—jiggling the mouth of the machine and shaking it from the base—to get the machine to deliver two, sometimes even three, gumballs at once. I knew you weren't supposed to swallow gum. It stayed in your stomach for seven years. That's what my mom had told me. But the taste of it was so sweet, I couldn't resist. As soon as it cracked open in my mouth, I wanted it to be a part of me.

Across the street from the hotel was a hot spring where people gathered to throw coins into the warm, dark water and make a wish. Beneath its rippling surface, you could see the cemetery of coins, the gleam of metal. All those wishes. I wondered how many of them had come true. My mom would take me to that hot spring to throw a coin in when she got off work some afternoons. She worked there, at the Arlington, as the banquet manager, setting up luncheons and parties for companies from Little Rock to Fort Smith. Leaving home in the morning, she looked the part of a working woman: flowing black slacks and a white blouse with buttons and an enormous collar, and her hair tied up in a chignon, held tight with hair spray.

I went back there once, as a grown-up, and the piano looked weathered and tuneless, the arcade games gone dim from neglect. But in my memory, it is all perfect. The way my mom and I wanted it to be.

My grandparents lived in Hot Springs, and so my mother, brother, and I had come there, from Kansas, where I was born, to be a family again. That's what my mom said, anyway. And maybe we were, for a little while. On Saturday mornings my grandpa would pick me and my brother, Clinton, up in his two-door truck and we would go for long drives through the hills to look for turtles, and if we found one, we would bring her back and put her in the little pond in the front yard of my grandparents' house. The house was on the top of the hill, big and brick, three stories high, and in the mists of the morning the pond had fog billowing above it that made it look like something from a fairy tale.

I wasn't allowed to go down to the pond by myself, because there were water moccasins that slithered on its shores—big, venomous cottonmouth snakes—which, of course, made it more exciting. I wanted to shoot a water moccasin with my slingshot, to watch it squirm and wriggle away. Maybe all little boys see danger and want, desperately, to be a part of it, or maybe I just wanted it more than other kids; I don't know. But in the back of my grandfather's truck, Clinton's arm wrapped around me, the stoic face of the turtle we'd found retreating under her shell in defeat, the long dirt road dipping and twisting to the horizon before us, I felt certain that I was going somewhere. That life was going to be an adventure.

My dad had come back to Arkansas not long after we'd arrived there, showing up like a ghost at the front door of the house we were renting a few miles away from my grandparents. It was always like this when they got back together. We'd be in the living room, playing, and my mom would suddenly be in the doorway, her eyes glinting from his familiar flame. She was terrified, but she was also excited. She yearned for his flames. "Go to the neighbors' house," she would say, the sound catching in her throat. "Go out the back before your dad sees you."

She must have been so tired of drinking wine that when that glass of whiskey walked through the door, she couldn't resist. At the sight of him you could see the car chase playing out in her eyes. She was afraid for us—for our well-being. But she also needed us gone so they could rip the house apart. Not long after he came back to town, he moved in with us.

They'd met in a rehab in Texas, then escaped together, got married, and rode off into the sunset. It was the Bonnie-and-Clyde story she could never stop reliving. He'd been married five times before, and already had three children, one with each of three of those wives—Billy, Joshua, and Julie, all of whom I would meet when I was older.

My mom had never been married but already had two kids of her own, with two different men—my sisters Summer, who was thirteen years older than me, and Meadow, who was seven years older. My sisters resented the way my dad treated my mom so much that after a few months of living with them together, Summer and Meadow went to live with my grandparents, which meant I didn't see them all that often.

When he was home, my dad would sit in his recliner with a big plastic gas-station jug full of sweet tea and extra ice, made with Sweet & Low that came in the pink packets. I watched the smile on my brother's face when my dad walked into the room; he'd jump straight into his lap. Clinton was always smiling. I didn't understand. I thought I should play sports, because I knew dads liked it when their sons were good at sports, and so I did that, all the time, but he never seemed to care. "Daddy loves his boys," he said, but the whiskey on his breath made it smell like a lie. Through an open window, fireflies glittered in the steamy air.

My life of crime started in broad daylight. The grown-ups would be gone. Clinton was watching *Star Trek* in the living room. So I would sneak out through the open garage and tiptoe to the neighbors' house, slipping in through the sliding door, my glasses fogged from the humidity. The excitement I felt was unparalleled—would they catch me coming in? Part of me wanted to get caught so I could get in trouble, which would mean attention.

Not far from the neighbors' door was the freezer. As I tugged it open, I felt the blast of cold air on my face, evaporating the condensation on my glasses. *Did they know I was doing this?* Inside was a rainbow sea of shaved-ice popsicles. I didn't care what color I got. Just the sugar rush, the gluttonous high of peeling the wrappers off with my teeth. Red, purple, blue, green. From start to finish, it was pure satisfaction.

Were they home? Did they pretend not to notice the little boy with dirt on his face and a shirt streaked with melted popsicles, rooting around in their freezer? It was euphoric. My little secret. Just seeing how long I could go until I got caught, which would be its own reward—the attention I was craving. But they never caught me in the act, and they kept replenishing the popsicles, time after time.

Other people's belongings were just plain better than mine—all the beautiful things other people had. I gravitated toward things tucked away in the darkness of a closet or cabinet, discarding what was mine and collecting what wasn't. I found a pair of my sister Meadow's sandals—lime-green and strappy with a chunky, rectangular heel. Plastic and sparkly, the texture of a translucent jump rope shot through with glitter. But my mom's closet was best of all. It was a secret treasure chest, like it was illuminated from the inside out, and it was as if celestial music started playing when I opened the doors to reveal all those shoes, and all those dresses. I wondered if other boys felt this way about their mothers' clothes. I wished I were a girl.

One afternoon I was in her closet, tottering around her bedroom in her shoes—worn-in leather boots, coffee brown, with a square toe and a thick three-inch heel—when she found me. She looked momentarily confused, then that expression changed to a kind of satisfaction, like I'd confirmed something she'd already known—and like it was a relief that she had been the one to discover this, and not my father. But instead of reprimanding me, she laughed. "I don't need another person fighting over my closet, Lou Lou," she said. "I already have two daughters."

That night, people were over—my sisters, their friends, and a few neighbors. We were all sprawled out on the burgundy carpet, some of the adults crowded on the lip of the old brick fireplace, above which hung a framed photograph of a Native American woman with long, pin-straight, jet-black hair with a feather in the back. There was a look of fear and lust on her face, like you couldn't tell if she was about to get fucked, murdered, or both. It was the same look I saw in my mother's eyes whenever my father came back.

I was dancing to the sound of TLC's "Creep" on the radio, twisting and shimmying, when someone yelled, "Colton, you're such a good dancer!"

"You should see him do it in heels," my mom said. I looked up at her—trying to figure out if she was angry, or encouraging, or both. But she just nodded at me, her beaded chandelier earrings dipping. So I ran to her room, retrieving the high-heeled boots and a big pendant necklace, slipping it around my neck and tugging the heels on. When I came back into the living room, everyone whooped and hollered as I recreated moves I'd seen in the music video, my heels a few inches higher, my soul lost in the melody. Had I ever been more myself? Will I ever be again?

It could have been that she wanted me to do it before my dad got home—so I could have that moment of disinhibition, without anyone's judgment. The possibility of getting found out, of getting caught, of getting seen for what I was—the danger of it. The thrill of it.

After everyone had gone home, she called me into her bedroom. "C'mere, Fat Butt," she said. "Come help me with my curlers." She called me anything but my actual name: Fat Butt, Lou Lou, Bucket Head, Fibber McGee. She was stupid gorgeous. Frighteningly beautiful. A Texas girl, a California girl, a bombshell. In my memory, her eyeliner is always smudged, a little cakey. As she rolled each ringlet of her long box-dyed brown hair around a curler, I slid a pin through it to hold it in place. I loved her more than the sun in the sky. I loved her more than ranch dressing. I loved her more than thinking about myself.

"You know how angry your dad gets with me when I start to get a little unbuttoned?" she said. I nodded, trying not to burn my fingers on the searing-hot curlers. But I always did. "Well, you're a boy. And boys aren't supposed to act that way." Our eyes met in the mirror above her dresser. "Imagine what he would do to you if he caught you acting like your sisters."

He had never done to me the things that he did to her. By the time he was ready to leave again, it wasn't like a movie—where the abused woman has a scrape, or a black eye. When my dad was finished with my mom she was purple and black. By the time we'd wake up, my dad would be long gone, leaving Clinton and me to pick up the mess he'd created. Bruises that became scars on my memory. We'd say we didn't miss him. But I was the only one who meant it. My mom was lost without him, and when he was gone, she was always searching for him. We all felt it—the way his absence made her rudderless.

I can remember slipping outside through the swinging screen door, into the backyard in Hot Springs, where the night was simmering. Fireflies fizzed around my bowl-cut hair. I caught one in my hand, then tightened my fist until I knew it was dead. Crushed in my palm now was a phosphorescent ooze. I smeared it over my face. I was a boy. I would glow in the dark all night.

CARLSBAD, NEW MEXICO
1994

The first time Uncle Tommy came to town, I was six and we were living in the Den House, which even today is still the name my siblings and I use when we talk about it, maybe because it was the only time we ever felt like a normal family. And I thought a normal family should have a den, the way families did on the sitcoms I used to watch. A separate room to play video games, to tell stories, to gather for some shared activity—this marked us as normal. This meant that things were going well.

I was in the den with Clinton when I heard the doorbell ring. Then my uncle Tommy was in the living room, and my mother was jumping into his arms. It was as if she would rather have been married to him, my father's brother—that's how beautiful he made her feel. She was happier than I'd ever seen her. Tommy was tall and lanky—he looked a little bit like Gumby. His legs were long in his tight blue Levi's. He was wearing a collared baby-blue shirt and had brown Bob Ross curls. He had come from Las Vegas, where he lived, to visit. He was happy, energetic, and sparkly, like Richard Simmons. I'd never met him before, but somehow he shifted naturally into uncle mode. He was comfortable around children. He knew how to be. I remember hanging from his neck, lying in the grass with him play-wrestling, everybody gathered around telling stories. And I remember my father, scowling in the doorway, as if he was irritated by this extension of him—his blood, his kin—who everyone seemed to favor over him. My father was always a shade of red. Even if he was smiling, it felt like someone had just turned on the heat in the house.

Garage sale signs on our unkempt front lawn, the same way it was every year. We had left Arkansas because our lease was up, or because my dad had gotten a job, selling used cars at Phil Carrell Chevrolet Buick—you said the whole name, just like that—in Carlsbad, New Mexico. Or maybe he'd moved out there without her, and my mom had followed him. They did this dance for so many years it's hard to remember what happened when. My sister Summer had made it to college in Arkansas, and Meadow had stayed behind in Hot Springs with my grandparents to finish high school.

Carlsbad was the place where I'd have my first brush with fame, starring alongside Clinton as the Phil Carrell Chevrolet Buick boys in a local commercial. We sang the jingle: "Phil Carrell

Chevrolet Buick—you can count on us!" Then we grinned. Both of us were missing our front teeth, which the tooth fairy had given us good value for.

This was the last time my parents would be together. Whatever effect my father had on women was the same effect my mother had on men. They were mirrors of each other: charismatic, intoxicating, and manipulative. They would drive each other to ruin, and they did it with gusto. You could see in my mom's eyes that she loathed being a homemaker, resented it on some deep and primal level. I always imagined her trying to cook dinner, then smashing a glass and going for my father's neck with it. In one of the best photographs of my parents together, they're both smiling—but they both have broken noses, like a real-life *Mr. and Mrs. Smith.* We didn't eat meals together as a family. We weren't that kind of family.

She cleaned, though. She was always cleaning, trying to keep herself busy, as if she thought she would please my dad by doing the things he thought a woman should do. Everything we had was old, but there was never a speck of dust on anything, even if everything had a sepia tint to it, as if it had been yellowed by age. It wasn't dirty, but it also wasn't clean. I don't remember her lavishing me with affection, the way parents did on TV, but our bond was still incredibly close; she probably gave me lots of words of affirmation that I've forgotten, but mostly I felt competitive with Clinton. He was so smart—always getting straight A's. And he was a clown, a ham—like a little Jim Carrey, doing impressions. He was lovable and affectionate. I craved attention, then ran away from it, so I never felt important.

But Uncle Tommy made me feel important. We were in the backyard, under the enormous piñon tree, and it must have been nighttime, because I was looking up at the string light that hung from the roof, and when I looked over at Tommy he was looking at me in a different way, in a way that no grown-up had looked at me before. We were on metal folding chairs, the kind with multicolored rubber strips forming the seat, like a beach ball, and I remember the feeling of the plastic under me as Tommy started touching his bulge through his jeans. I was excited by it. I was six; I didn't know it was wrong. I remember putting my hand on the bulge, and soon his pants were unbuttoned. And then I remember licking it, because I couldn't fit it in my mouth.

I knew that little boys weren't supposed to do things like this. I knew this was what girls did with boys. Did he tell me that it was our secret, that I shouldn't tell anyone? If he did, I don't remember it—but somehow I knew, instinctively, never to tell. It was too exciting, too dangerous. It created a series of new sensations that sent chills down my leg. I wondered if we would get caught. The feeling of it was supposed to be bad, but instead it felt so good. We had shared something. I had never met anyone before whom I could share that with. We had the same weird hidden light, a secret, a gift.

When Tommy left town, I don't remember being sad. I felt grateful that he had come to arm me with a superpower. He had seen me; he had noticed me. I didn't know what beauty was, other than the way that I saw my mom. This was the first time I had ever felt wanted. Doing things like that—sex things—was going to give me that sensation again, the feeling of being desired, the feeling of getting someone else's attention.

How do you understand something like this as a child? You can't; you don't. I could have blamed my parents, whose lust for chaos left me vulnerable. Or I could have blamed Tommy, the perpetrator. But instead I blamed myself. The things Tommy taught me, I thought, would help me along in my slithering deviant life. I wasn't dirty, but I also wasn't clean. I was just the way certain animals were, like the water moccasins in my grandparents' pond.

The first boy I remember falling in love with was named Brice, a boy in the same grade as me. He was small and towheaded and always laughing.

That—his laughter—did something to me. When I saw people experience emotion so purely—like genuine, unadulterated joy—I was overcome with envy. If I was bouncing a basketball, or playing in the yard, I'd stop just to watch someone laugh. *Why can't that be me?* I wondered. I wasn't happy unless I was alone, lost in the world I was creating for myself. When I was playing with a ball, or throwing rocks at oncoming traffic, or doing anything alone, I was at peace. Nobody was telling me how to do things, or to act a certain way.

In his closet after school, Brice and I played our favorite game—show-and-tell. "Okay," he said, "I'll do that as long as you don't pee in my mouth." I liked the shame that came afterward. It felt like a natural way to keep me from craving the feeling again too soon.

They didn't fight in front of us, but it always started the same way. My father's red face would get even redder. Then the sound of a door slamming. That was like an invitation—like when my mom slammed a door, she was inviting him in. *Let the games begin, Bill.*

Then shouting. An exasperated scream from my mom, like the wind had just been knocked out of her. She had bloodlust. She wasn't drunk, or if she was, I wasn't aware of it. She just wanted to feel something. In the other bunk bed in our room, Clinton would be crying. He was usually the happiest kid I'd ever seen. But once their shouting started, the joy drained from my brother's face. He would weep at a volume that was impossible to ignore. He knew that if they heard him, it was likelier that they would stop fighting, or at least fight more quietly.

Even then, I was already so much like them. Clinton wasn't. Clinton was better. Even though I was younger, I felt protective of his innocence. But at the same time, I was jealous of the attention he got. I wanted to shield him from the unkindness of the world—which I seemed to see, when he saw the best in everyone—but I also didn't want him to get the spotlight instead of me.

When my dad was around, I felt like I was in a shell. It was as if I had to lock those heels back up in the closet and wait for the day he'd leave so I could put them on again.

My dad moved to the other side of town, to an apartment in a neighborhood called San José, but we called it San-Jo. Not long after, my mom moved us out of the house with the den, which we couldn't afford anymore, to an apartment behind a roller rink called Blades where I liked to skate, a few blocks away from where my dad was living. Things were different in that part of town—the smell of dry, hot orange clay and kush, the sight of dirty heroin rigs and used condoms on the ground when I walked home from school, men in oversized red hoodies, peering out of tinted car windows.

My parents kept trying to work things out, even though it always ended exactly the same way. It was as though they just loved breaking each other's heart.

A woman named Margaret lived in the same apartment complex as my dad. They both worked at the used car lot, where she was a receptionist, and soon they began dating. In her late forties, Margaret had a frost-gray bouffant and caked-on foundation that always looked slightly cracked, and she was painfully thin. Her waist was exactly twenty-four inches, which I knew because she used to wrap a brown woven belt around her waist like a corset to measure it. "Bill likes me to stay trim," she said.

They smoked hash together, and there were always pill bottles around—oxycodone, hydrocodone. Margaret wasn't as beautiful as my mom, but there was something about her. She looked like she probably had a gun in her handbag at all times. She taught me how to wash my hair in the sink.

"That twig bitch," my mom said. She took a swig of the Natty Light she'd poured into a tall glass. She had started drinking more heavily. "Your dad thinks he picked a good girl, but she's trashier than all the rest of them." I nodded. I knew that I wasn't supposed to, but I couldn't help it—I liked Margaret. She didn't seem to mind the way I was, when I was over at her apartment when my dad wasn't around, dancing and acting a little more girlish.

And most of all, I liked her son, Jason. He had auburn hair, the color of a piece of furniture that had been bleached by the sun, and freckles all over his body. He was the kind of kid who people talked about—the kind of kid every parent worries about. He was a little arsonist—he liked to throw lit matches at people and had already been to a juvenile detention center. I would never have acted out like that, but I understood the impulse: to burn things down just to see what would happen.

I started spending more time at my dad's, or at Margaret's. I pretended it was so I could spend more time with my dad, but it was actually to see Jason. Under the same roof, I wouldn't have to sneak around. I wouldn't have to dive into dark places to find that light. He was always right there.

When I spent the night at Margaret's, Jason and I would fall asleep on the floor in the living room, watching movies. My dad had already retreated to the bedroom, while Margaret took off her makeup and reapplied a more natural face in case my dad woke from slumber. It was always the same: sliding hands, sweaty palms, moving our feet toward each other, slowly, in an attempt to touch toes. We were children. We didn't know what we were doing, but we knew what we wanted.

One day we were at my dad's apartment, completely naked, when we both looked up to see Margaret in the doorway. She looked stricken, her pale face now rouged from rage. "Put your god-damn clothes on," she said. "And get the fuck out here."

In a panic, we dressed and went to the living room for what-ever punishment we were going to face, which I knew would surely be world ending. As we stood in front of Margaret, the door opened and my father walked in. And if Margaret, or any woman he was with, didn't have a gas-station-sized jug of sweet tea waiting for him the moment he arrived home, it was going to be a week of psychological terror. So she ran to grab him his sweet tea, and kissed him on the mouth. As she turned back to us, I saw some frustration graze her face. She hadn't had time to primp for him, which must have bothered her; she cared so much what other people thought of her. He would've killed us, and her, if he knew what she'd seen. So she said nothing. And we never spoke of it again.

When we had to move away again, I knew I wouldn't see Jason anymore.

When I was eight, my mom found a house out in the country, where the landlord cut her a deal if she agreed to take care of an aging horse that lived in a stable on the property. It was the high desert of New Mexico, scrubbed by the sun. All the crops looked yellow and dead. I began having night terrors, demonic visions where I was very small and being chopped up or locked in a trunk, and I would wake up screaming and hyperventilating, scratching myself with my fingernails. My mom would comfort me: "Come here, baby." And then, like a party trick, she would whip out, seemingly from nowhere, a glass of freezing cold water and pour it in my face. She had figured out that the shock of the cold water was the only thing that would snap me out of the horrific visions. I wept and wailed. In my memory I can't see the dreams themselves, but I see a supercut of that: The cold water hitting my face. My head hitting the pillow. Wondering if I would ever be normal.

Around that same time, men started spending the night at the house. They revolved in and out, never staying long. They were uniformly ugly, and they paid some of my mom's bills, which she had a bad habit of tearing up, unopened. She wrote hot checks, too, and usually got away with it. People must have wondered: *Who is this woman? She's so beautiful, so kind, and so sweet.* Finally, it caught up with her, and she was sentenced to two days in county jail.

Normally, when my mom disappeared, I didn't know that she was leaving, so I didn't have time to prepare for the stress of her abandonment, but this time, I knew she was going away. As she left for her stint in jail, I realized it was the first time I'd seen her leave the house without makeup. She always curled her hair. She loved luxuriating in getting ready; it was glamorous to her. I remember thinking, *She doesn't leave the house like this.* But she was smart enough not to show up to jail looking like a beauty queen.

She stationed the man she was dating to stay with us while she served her time. His name was Cecil, and he was an animal control officer. He had a nasal voice, like a character on *The Simpsons*, with ginger-red hair and a porno mustache and an olive-green uniform, but he was kind. When I woke up in a cold sweat that night, I wept in Cecil's arms, and I remember wrapping myself around him and inhaling his smell of stale cigarettes. It was so comforting; it reminded me of my mom. That smell lived in her hair no matter how much Aqua Net she used.

Everyone knew my family was troubled. We had weekly check-ins from social services, who must have had a file an inch thick on us from all the times my mom almost lost my sisters.

At school, everyone assumed I was being beaten because I'd show up with scratch marks I'd given myself when I was sleeping. Violence did have a way of following us around. Right in front of the San José Catholic Church, we got into a car accident so bad that Clinton had to be taken away in an ambulance. I rode with him in the back, as blood streamed out of his face, and he kept asking, "Is this a dream? Is this a dream?" He had to get 150 stitches on one side of his face. While he was recovering, kids at school called him Scarface. I got suspended three times for hitting kids who called him that.

Walking home from school one day, I saw the antique wicker baskets my mom kept on the wall flying out the front door, bouncing on the wild watermelons that grew in the front yard. And, like in an action movie, Meadow and my mom tumbled out the front door, pummeling each other. My mom was grabbing my sister's long blond hair, pulling at it, and both of them were screaming. My sister's frustration over constantly being displaced had reached a boiling point. She was finally old enough to express her anger in a physical way, and my mom had a special talent for egging her on.

In my memory, I go back to the Den House. To the photographs of my seventh birthday party. I was so excited that day. I was wearing big glasses and acid-washed shorts, and I had no shirt on, because I hadn't learned to hate my body yet.

My mom loved parties. They weren't lavish; everything was from the Dollar Store. There were triangle streamers in pastel colors strung over the kitchen table, which had a brightly colored tablecloth over it, and it felt fancy and important. I could see from the joy in her eyes that she was excited to put it together for me. I wished every day were a party, just for that sight alone. She was wearing a color-blocked sweater, dark maroon and turquoise. I had asked for a vanilla cake with chocolate frosting, and I didn't want to share it with anyone. I'm sure we were listening to Selena or Mariah Carey—because I always was.

A piñata had been strung from the tree in the yard. My mom put the blindfold on me and spun me around a couple of times. I was so athletic, I knew I would hit it immediately. But in the dark, I was disoriented. I swung and felt myself striking against the air. Distantly, I heard a few snickers from the guests—the other kids, neighbors, and family who had gathered. I grounded down in my feet and swung again, but by that point, I'd lost my balance. I felt myself dip, like I was going to topple over. I could hear kids laughing louder now. What if I wasn't as good as I thought I was? I swung a third time, but missed again. That was it—now it was someone else's turn. I tore off the blindfold to see another kid break the piñata on the first try.

It wasn't fair. I ripped the T-ball bat from his hands. I swung it at the piñata. The turquoise and mustard papier-mâché tore open. A pack of Smarties fell out, then another. I swung the bat at it again and the whole thing cracked open. Tears were streaming down my face, although I didn't know why. It must have been clear to everyone that I was having a tantrum. Kids fell to the floor, grasping for the candy, and I began grabbing it out of their hands. I wanted it all. It was my birthday. None of it was fair—none of it.

It wasn't until I went back and looked at the photographs that I saw Tommy in the background, in his tight jeans and his mop of curls, smiling for the camera, his hands on my shoulders. I'm not smiling. In photos from my birthday the year before, and the year before that, I was grinning my little-boy grin with my cake and my mom. But not in the pictures from the house with the den.

Not long after we moved out of the rental with the elderly horse, my mom met a man named Charlie. Our new landlord. He was tall, a little chubby, and handsome, and he treated my mom like a queen. He was my favorite. He ate jalapeños with every meal, taught me how to play dominoes with his buddies, and introduced me to rap music on long drives to test out the volume capacity of his ever-changing sound system. I wanted him to be my real dad. He kept a stack of *Playboy* magazines under his bed. I loved the women in those magazines, even if I didn't find them arousing. They had no scars. They were beautiful. They didn't have to cover up. The way men talked about women—I wanted to be talked about that way. I wanted to be desired.

It was clear that people wanted sex.

I wondered how I could get men to feel that way about me.

3

ANDALE, KANSAS
1998

I woke up just as we crossed the border from Oklahoma into Kansas, and the sun was bright in the back seat of the car. There was sweat puddling under my cheek on the leather seat. My mom couldn't drive at night. She used to tell me it was because she was afraid of falling asleep at the wheel, but it was probably because she was drinking. I was in the back of the '87 Datsun station wagon she'd managed to buy after trading in our old life in Carlsbad, and there was no air-conditioning, because there was never air-conditioning, and already the day was sticky. The car felt like a kiln.

"Pull over, I'm feeling carsick," I called from the back seat.

"What?" she hollered back. Next to me, Clinton stirred.

"I'm gonna throw up," I said. Exasperated, I felt the whirring of the engine as she switched lanes. I leaned my head back and tried to hold it in. *One, two, three, four . . .*

At a truck stop, stumbling out the door, I vomited onto the concrete. I looked up to see my mom rolling her eyes. Why was everything I did such an inconvenience to everyone? Why wouldn't anyone believe me when I said I was sick, or unhappy, instead of thinking I was just being dramatic all the time?

As I clambered back into the car, I looked around at the fields that surrounded us for miles in every direction. It was so different from the landscape of New Mexico, the barrenness of the desert. Here it was lush but yellow, like the sun was shining from below.

"Where do all the people live?" I asked. "Where are all the houses?" I leaned over the center console. My nose was in my mother's hair, which smelled like Shalimar and TRESemmé TRES. Extra-hold. Nonaerosol.

"If you walk in the middle of those fields," she said, pointing, and my eyes followed her finger, "there." She motioned to the perfectly cut rows of grain, then put her hand on my chest. "That's where the homes are." Was she trying to tell me that home is where the heart is? She did this sometimes—speaking in riddles, wanting us to put the pieces together for ourselves. Then she lit a cigarette.

"Come on, Fat Butt," she said. "We're gonna be late to see Uncle Mike."

Mike's house sat between two large milo fields. Two stories under an unfinished roof, it stuck out against the horizon, a blight. He'd built it himself, but had abandoned the project years ago after making just one floor of the house habitable when the workload of the farm became too much for him. For as long as I could remember, my mom had threatened to send us to live with him when we were acting up.

"I'm sending you to the farm!" she'd yell.

"No!" I screamed. "I promise I'll be good!" I didn't know exactly what happened on the farm, but if it was a consequence for whatever I'd been doing, it had to be unpleasant.

"You boys think your lives are so terrible," she said, stubbing out a cigarette. "You'll learn once Uncle Mike puts you to work on the farm." Now that my dad was seeing Margaret, there had been no reason to stay in New Mexico anymore. She couldn't be in the same town with him, she said; not even in the same state. It was too upsetting for her to watch my dad settle and continue to take the easy way out. So we packed up our life yet again, said goodbye to Charlie, and headed toward Uncle Mike's farm in Kansas.

He greeted us at the top of the driveway. "Dana!" he said to my mom, embracing her. He feigned confusion at the sight of me and my brother, making a joke at how much we'd grown. "Have you seen Clinton and Colton? Here, let me ask these two young men."

Mike had been common-law married to my mom's sister, my aunt Cassie, for over a decade. They had since separated, and Cassie now lived forty minutes away in Wichita, but Mike was still part of the family. He was in charge of circulation for the local newspaper. His eyes were kind and blue, and he was smiling underneath his graying lumberjack beard. The wind carried me into his arms and I tugged on the navy bandanna that his long brown hair was tucked beneath. "Colton, quit it," he chuckled. His childlike voice felt like a gift.

Instead of a place where children went to be tortured, the farm turned out to be magical. It was so far from the other homes you couldn't see any neighbors, and the house was surrounded by a sea of rusted old trucks Mike had long given up on fixing. We tripped over animals of every kind—puppies, chickens, kittens, and a mean billy goat. An old jungle gym. An abandoned barn. Mike let everyone draw on the walls of the house in markers, in different colors; there were little snatches of poetry and crude drawings from anyone who had come to visit. And, most importantly, there was space. For a kid, there could be no greater paradise. The chaos of Carlsbad—where we'd been woken up one night by gunshots and the news that our next-door neighbor had been murdered—felt far away. Things would be different here. I was sure of it.

Andale, Kansas, was a tranquil town of about six hundred people. At first, it scared me that there were no speed limit signs running alongside the cratered dirt roads, but soon I realized it was an invitation: to drive fast and free. The happy-seeming families playing tag on their front lawns—maybe we could be a family like that, finally, now that we were far away from my dad. When you drove, the dirt roads spat up so much dust, it would betray your location from a mile away. The koozie cups kept your drinks so cold, you barely noticed it was summertime. John Deere tractors made the hourly trips to the only feedlot in town. People seemed happy. People smiled. Summerfest. Trampolines. Catholic church. Main Street. Friday night football. Blue-eyed blondes meeting up with their high school sweethearts, the girls in flip-flops, the boys in shit-kickers. Clouds as unvaryingly white as the people below them.

In New Mexico, I had always been terrified of the weather. When the rain came, I hid in my mother's arms, hid under beds, hid in closets. But the first time a storm came to Andale, it felt different.

You could sense when a tornado was starting to form. First there was a stillness in the air. The humidity would rise. Looking out the window, over those long, flat fields that went on for miles, it looked as if fog was rolling in. As the storm gathered, there were cirrus clouds—thin and gray and transparent, like cigarette smoke. Then as they grew nearer, they became cumulonimbus clouds, as white and solid as a thought bubble in a cartoon. Before long there were funnel clouds, black and shelflike. And that's when the sirens began to wail. They rattled in my head, even from far away—we were five miles outside town, but somehow the sound cut through the distance. You heard them in your body. You turned the TV on to KAKE-10, the local news, where the meteorologist would be showing the map of the counties at risk. Hail the size of softballs would pelt down from the sky, smashing car windows and bouncing on the fields. And as the tornado approached, there was an eerie sound on the wind, almost like a train bleating its horn, and then the air, which was moments ago humid, was suddenly cold. But if the power went out, you couldn't turn to the news to tell you where the storm was, so you had to count it: As the clouds began producing thunder, you could time the seconds between the thunder and the strike of lightning, which would tell you how many miles away the storm was.

Something about the fear was different here: the rush of the unexpected, the intensity of the terror. It felt as thrilling as a roller-coaster ride. How can I describe the exhilaration of seeing my first tornado? I was looking out the window from the second story of Uncle Mike's house, and it felt like it was destined for me, the endless dark swirl around the axis of it, furious and inevitable. In the distance, farms were uprooted. Pieces of roof blew through the air. People's lives were being torn apart in real time. Would that be us someday? I wondered. How could something so beautiful be so destructive? It stopped me dead in my tracks. The way they worked in unity—the chaos and the calm. As soon as it was over, I wanted to know when it would happen again. Watching it gave me an amazing feeling.

After the thunderstorms, the ditches that ran through town would fill up with rainwater, and people would float down them in inner tubes, like traveling in gondolas along the canals of Venice. I had never known what I wanted to do with my life until this point. Now, if anybody asked me what I wanted to be when I grew up, I could tell them.

I wanted to be a storm chaser.

Kids were different in Andale. In New Mexico, they dressed in baggy JNCO jeans, hoodies emblazoned with Tommy Hilfiger logos, and Fila sneakers. In Andale, I went to Catholic school, where we wore uniforms: shirts in white, navy blue, or baby blue, and khaki pants. We all looked clean, wholesome. Everyone seemed to love sports the way I did: Basketball was everyone's obsession, and I was lucky enough to have moved there in time to sign up for a summer league team. The first time I played in Andale, my mom came to watch my game. I was so excited that I shot a three-pointer at the wrong hoop, almost scoring against my own team.

The teachers were nicer too. They seemed genuinely interested in me, laughing with me, looking for ways to give me extra credit. So I'd come to school early and stock the fridge with chocolate milk, pass out papers, use the janitor's massive broom to sweep the gym floor before PE, color-code the dodgeballs for the next class, sharpen pencils, and clean the chalkboards. I remember thinking it was ridiculous that I was getting extra credit for this—it was so easy, surely I was taking advantage of their generosity—but I loved the feeling it gave me, that I was useful and reliable.

My homeroom teacher, and my favorite teacher, was Mr. Lyon. He was stocky, had a face like a Rottweiler, and coached the basketball team. His classroom was decorated in Carolina blue and white, the colors for his favorite college team, the North Carolina Tar Heels, its walls covered in UNC memorabilia. I had been desperate for him to take a liking to me, and it didn't take much time before he did—the first time he took attendance in class, when he reached my name, he smiled a shit-eating grin. "Colton Haynes," he said. "Hope you plan on shooting at the right basket in practice later." How did he hear about that? Were people talking about me already? The class erupted into laughter, and so did I, wanting to be in on the joke. It didn't matter if I was now eternally known as the kid who shot at the wrong basket. It made me feel like I was the teacher's pet, just in time for tryouts that year.

The middle school gym had an old wooden floor that was lacquered to a brilliant shine, that fresh-start feeling that cleared every scoreboard from seasons past. Empty bleachers along the east side wall—I imagined them filled up with people, cheering me on.

Immediately after school, I rushed to change in the locker room so I would be the first one on the court. I imagined Mr. Lyon showing up to witness me dribbling the basketball between my legs and seeing me hit shots from well beyond the three-point line, but my showboating was cut short by his whistle. "Give me fifty suicides without stopping, ladies!"

"Yes, sir!"

"You ladies will never live up to last year's A team. You gonna prove me wrong?"

"Yes, sir!"

"Are you calling me a liar?"

"No, sir!"

Sweat dripped down my clavicle as I darted from baseline and back, free-throw line and back, three-point line and back, half-court line and back, then the same on the opposing side of the court. The bigger boys who played center fell out first, then the shooting guards, until the battle of the point guards began. I was more of a shooting guard myself, but I wanted to show my speed. I had a desperate need to impress him. But as the warm-up came to a close, I ran out of fuel and collapsed.

Mr. Lyon stomped toward me in his Jordan Retro 5s. I couldn't look him in the eye. I knew I had let him down.

"I thought you were mister hotshot," he barked. "Can you hear me? Are your ears open?" I nodded. I felt like a fraud. This was always the pattern with me—craving attention from older men, then feeling, somehow, like I wasn't enough, or I had fallen short of their expectations of me. I'd wanted to be seen, but in that moment I wished I were invisible.

Mike and my mom were extremely close and stayed up late partying together most nights. They had history: The impression he made on her was so strong when they first met that she pushed her C-section date to have me two days later, so Uncle Mike and I could share the same birthday. My dad was not happy about that.

My mom slept on the couch so Clinton and I could share a bedroom. But pretty soon, she was sleeping in Uncle Mike's room. In the mornings, her face would be smudged with last night's makeup. One day, she was watching us play from an abandoned trailer stoop that was on the property, sitting with her half-cracked beer and cigarette as we ran through the sprinklers in the yard. She was wearing blue jeans and a green tank top. Her skin was fresh and dewy. She pulled me into her arms. "You're happy here, aren't you, Lou Lou?" I nodded. "Good," she said. I knew she felt the same freedom there that I did. There was no one there to hurt her, or us. It was impossible to get in trouble.

Of course the situation was doomed; she was bound to get bored of it eventually, and the weather would have to turn. One morning, Clinton and I were startled awake by an unfamiliar sound—not the Willie Nelson or Donovan that was usually playing, but the sound of a loud, dull thud. It sounded like the hail that pelted down before a tornado, but it was just one repeated, pulsing strike. I ran to the window and saw my mom trying to beat the front door down with a baseball bat, wearing the studded motorcycle jacket she wore on nights out. She looked undone, like she had just woken up, or just gotten home—it was always hard to tell. Finally, Mike let her into the house. He was yelling, which we'd never heard before. He was the gentlest man, with the evenest keel—until his jealousy was activated, and it had been now. My mom had started sleeping with one of his paper delivery boys—a handsome twenty-five-year-old named Chris.

"You broke the door off the hinges," he yelled. "I was trying to help by putting a roof over your head and this is how you repay me?"

She was crying, inconsolable. "Keep it down," I heard her slur as they headed upstairs. "The boys are in the other room."

Within minutes of their arguing, there was another loud crash from the downstairs door and we could hear footsteps pounding up the stairs toward them. Clinton and I both darted out into the hallway and saw that Chris had arrived, and a fight had broken out among the three of them, with my mom caught between her two admirers. "Let her go!" Clinton screamed. "Don't hurt my mama!"

We were both sobbing. "Boys, go back in your room now," she wailed. We froze. "Go!" she yelled again. We tucked ourselves away, out of their direct eyeline, but still in view of the wreckage they were causing in the living room. In the melee, the delivery boy threw a punch at Mike, but instead it landed square in my mom's face. It sounded like a sandbag had been dropped from the second floor of the farmhouse as she fell in front of the couch, over the makeshift coffee table, while he ran downstairs and off the property. She stayed in that position, not moving. Eventually we got her up onto the couch, where she lay supine all day, covered under blankets. We let her rest.

The next morning, she was already up at the kitchen table with a cigarette and beer when I got up, the right side of her face swollen. She looked embarrassed, and furious, like she couldn't believe that someone had done that in front of her kids. In all these years, it was the first time I had ever actually seen a man hit her. And I knew, on some level, that she caused all this drama because she was itching to leave—she always was—but also was attached to the stability she'd imagined living with Mike had provided us. Now that had been revealed to be an illusion too.

"I don't want to be here anymore," I said. "Can't we live somewhere else?" The look on her face confirmed what I had suspected. It was as if she had been waiting for one of us to ask the question, to give her permission to abandon this semblance of home. She'd been squirming to escape it, but had been delaying for our benefit. Now, finally, she could leave again.

"Where?" she said. "Where would you be happy?"

"I like it here," I said. "In Andale."

"I do too," Clinton said.

"So can we go?" I asked.

"Yeah," she said. "I'll figure something out."

Mike bought the station wagon off her, and she used the money to buy a white Toyota Celica from a girl who was heading off to college in the fall, a girl whose daddy had bought her a brand-new car to take her to Kansas State. The idea of that—the wealth of it—was staggering to me.

After only three months, we packed up our things yet again and loaded them into the back of the car. As we sped away from Uncle Mike's farm, the sky overhead was clear and blue again, clouds of dirt spitting past the window as we bounced along the unpaved road. A white car wasn't practical in a town like this, but it was the best we could do. It was funny, the way storms rolled in, the way a sunny day could turn overcast on a dime. We were only moving four miles away, to the middle of town, and nothing was going to change besides leaving farm life behind, but it still felt like the end of something.

I looked at my mom, her jaw set in the driver's seat, her sunburned shoulders, her tangled hair. She was the tornado. In the wake of destruction, everything felt so clear.

4

ANDALE, KANSAS
2001

I remember his badge, shiny and gold.

I remember the way he looked standing in the hallway by the lockers, a baby-blue shirt tucked into tight black chinos. It almost looked like he had cuffed the sleeve so it would hook around his muscle, like he wanted me to see his arms, so it would make me want him. He was always tan from the Kansas sun, blue eyes—ocean eyes—and glimmering blond hair. When I look at pictures of him now, he doesn't do it for me, but at the time, he meant something. I couldn't even make eye contact with him. Looking at him made me feel the way I felt when I listened to my favorite boy bands, like I was waiting in line at Walmart for a new album to come out, wanting to hold it in my hands, to listen to every word.

I knew I was going to have him one day. His name was Damon.

He wasn't gay, at least not in the way I was beginning to suspect I was, even if I didn't have the words for it at the time. He helped run an afterschool program at the high school, where Clinton was already a student. And he was a cop in one of the surrounding towns, which I would have known from the way he stood up straight and looked people square in the eye, but when I watched him speed away in his cruiser with the decals all up the side, it felt like a movie.

The high school was next to the junior high, in an adjacent building. I was in seventh grade the first time we met. I went to see Clinton one day after school and Damon was there, and he looked at me and he smiled, not in a creepy way, but in a friendly, reassuring way, and I thought he looked like safety. He looked like how a man should be.

I liked the way his hair was blond at the tips. Frosted, they called it, like a cake, like sugar cereal—sweet. I went to the only store in town, Krause's, pacing up and down the vacant aisle, looking for an at-home kit to do that to myself, and when the cashier rang me up and I counted out eight dollars in cash, I felt brave, like I was at the beginning of something. In the cramped bathroom, looking at my reflection in the cracked mirror, plastic gloves bunched around my wrists, I watched as my hair changed color, turning golden in the light. I wanted it to turn me golden too.

At school the next day, it looked like his.

There was only one paved road going through Andale, and that was the street where we had moved after we left Mike's farm, to a two-bedroom apartment behind a storefront that housed an endless succession of failed businesses: First it had been a hair salon, then it was a tanning salon called the Sunny Spot, and then it sat vacant. The apartment looked garage-sale ready at all times—cluttered, yet tidy, and prepared for a move at a moment's notice. My mom sourced and repurposed old leather luggage, its texture creased and weathered, to use as an end table, with a thin plate of glass over it. She stacked yellowed paperbacks she would never read in neat piles on the floor. The walls were yellowed from smoke. A Curtis Mathes television set was plugged in but didn't work, so she bought another used television set that she stacked on top of it, using the nonoperational one as a TV stand. She had a knack for procuring old items that she dubbed valuable antiques and then selling them at her "antique shop" called the Dusty Trail. It wasn't a real shop—it was a booth at whatever swap meet she could find, in whatever city we were living in at the time. She even had a sign made that said The Dusty Trail that would travel in the car with us on our yearly moves.

My mom's sister, my aunt Cassie, had grown up watching *Antiques Roadshow* religiously with my grandma, and my mom and Cassie still never missed an episode. In the living room, they sniped back and forth.

"I told you, Dana, you have that wax lamp! The exact one!" Cassie crowed.

"God, shut up, Cassie! Why are you always talking during the show?"

I sat next to the TV, not watching it, but watching them. I'd be flipping through a magazine or skimming through a textbook for the keywords I'd be likely to see on the next day's test, which

I'd eventually write on my thigh just above my kneecap, praying I'd remember to wear my longer brown khaki uniform shorts on test day. I'd gotten in trouble for cheating before, but it was only when I wrote the words on my wrist—they'd never think to check my legs.

Mostly I was mesmerized by the way they watched television. Why, I wondered, would anyone bother watching someone inside a grainy picture when you could watch people in real life? But to my mom and Cassie, it was magical to watch the stories of everyday people having their fates transformed by what happened on the show—some getting less than they'd hoped, others getting prices that would change their lives forever. They were like two old pirates, appraising their fool's gold.

On the main street of Andale was a dive called the Little Bear, where my mom had gotten a job tending bar. Just past the front door, there was a neon sign in red with the name of the bar and a glowing outline of a grizzly bear. The space was long and narrow, and its walls were lined with championship plaques from the high school team's football victories, framed newspaper articles of the accomplishments of Andale's best-known families, and a photograph of the ribbon-cutting ceremony from the bar's opening decades prior. During the day, it was the town lunch spot, but at night, it was the only place in town to let loose, and on Coyote Ugly nights, my mom and the other local party girls would get fucked up and dance on the bar.

Every sandwich on the menu was named after a different bear. My favorite was the Brown Bear, a roast beef club with lettuce, tomato, and, critically, ranch dressing, of which I always ordered extra. The food was prepared in a makeshift kitchen behind the bar, which consisted mostly of four George Foreman grills. There were loose wires everywhere. A permit was proudly displayed at the entrance to the kitchen in case anyone questioned if it was up to code.

I was desperate to work there. It was the only place in town where people seemed truly uninhibited: People swore, smoke, sang karaoke, played Keno with tiny pencils that looked like they'd been slashed in half. At the Little Bear, my mom was wholly herself. Nobody told her what to do. Without her kids around, desperate for attention, she was liberated. Instead, adult men were the ones seeking her affection, and she meted it out like a maestro, teasing them, keeping them interested, even if she wouldn't sleep with them unless they had something meaningful to offer her family. She was damn good at her job. She was so alive, and everyone there loved her. She was a queen in her castle.

After I'd begged them relentlessly, the owners of the bar let me wash dishes in the kitchen, even though I was still too young. They paid me five dollars an hour, under the table, for three-hour shifts on two nights a week—Friday and Saturday—which netted out to thirty dollars a week. I missed every Friday night football game, and part of me wanted to be there instead—feeling the thrill of proximity to those boys in their gleaming white uniforms, the bright lights flashing overhead, instead of scrubbing grease from pots and pans in the back of a dingy kitchen. But it was a small price to pay to have a front-row seat to the show my mom put on every night.

After my shifts on Friday nights, I'd steal a case or two of beer from the walk-in refrigerator and leave them behind the dumpster for the high school kids to take to their parties. I knew it would earn their goodwill; eventually, they started letting me tag along.

Everyone knew my mom was a partier, but Clinton and I were still popular at school because everyone knew that we didn't have to follow any rules. Our household was the Wild West. When the bar closed at 2:00 a.m., my mom would drive home drunk, even though we lived only two blocks away, and if she found that we hadn't done our chores, she would put on Donovan, playing the same songs on repeat until we woke up to finish in the middle of the night. Even on school nights. Or she would talk on the phone until the sun came up, to her sister Cassie, or her friends Dorinda and Nano, who were back in New Mexico. Sometimes there was a man over, and the sounds they made kept us awake.

From the window of that apartment, I could see everything there was to see in Andale: the only grocery store in town, Krause's; a white water tower that had the town's name painted on it in dark blue letters; a massive grain silo; and the Little Bear. Across the street was an ATM and a liquor store, and next to that was a doctor's office and a barber shop. We didn't even have a gas station. The nearest one was ten miles away, so you needed enough gas to get there.

I played every sport I could, running eight miles a day for cross-country. Four miles before school and four miles after. I'd run for as long as I could, until it got too dark and it was time to go home, or to the Little Bear, where my mom would be behind the bar, a cold brown bottle in her hand, smiling at me with her verdant eyes when I walked through the door.

She was happy at the Little Bear, happy with our life in Kansas, away from my dad. He'd still show up every so often, when he and Margaret would temporarily break up, pulling into town in his used champagne Buick LeSabre to take out his frustration on her. Clinton and I would make ourselves scarce for a couple of hours so they could drink and fuck and fight, then come back to survey the wreckage. The last time he came to Andale, we interrupted them mid-fight. Clinton tried to intervene, pushing my dad into a cabinet. My dad was so drunk he just collapsed to the floor. "Go!" my mom yelled to us. "Get out of here!" We scrambled out the door. After we left, he threw her through a glass coffee table.

When she came home from the hospital, she was a mess of stitches and bruises. She looked embarrassed, as she always did. "I'm sorry," she whispered. "I'm so sorry you had to see that." Nobody at the Little Bear would have believed that she would let a man do that to her, so she lied about it. Weeks later, I overheard her telling a customer she'd gotten into a car accident. With everyone but my dad, she was fearless.

Clinton had a part-time job in the kitchen of a breakfast spot right across the street from the Little Bear, owned by a conservative couple who were prominent in Andale. The matriarch of the family, Karen, was a polished, God-fearing woman; my mom thought she was an uppity bitch. When my mom heard that Karen had said something disparaging about her, the next time Karen came into the Little Bear, my mom punched her in the face. The next day, Karen fired my brother. In retaliation, my brother put a rock in a box, wrote BOOM! on it, and placed it on their doorstep. The bomb squad was called.

Clinton managed to stay out of juvie and got sentenced to nine months of curfew, where he was effectively under house arrest after 6:00 p.m. My mom wasn't angry at Clinton—she thought it was funny. "Karen should have kept my name out of her mouth," she said. "Nosy twat."

I was thirteen years old when people started talking about the way I looked. It was the summer before high school, and I had graduated with short hair, but I grew it out so it was long and swooped in the front, like Zac Efron in *High School Musical*. That wasn't the reference my mom preferred; she wanted me to let it grow long like Mick Jagger, but we both agreed it was an improvement. I had started looking in the mirror the way Clinton did—mussing up my hair, clenching my jaw when my mouth was closed, and sucking in my cheeks when it was open the way I'd heard Tyra Banks say the girls should do on *America's Next Top Model*. Not long before school started for the year, I saw some girls from my class. "Colton, I didn't even recognize you," one of them said. I had gone from uniforms into wearing hand-me-down American Eagle and Aeropostale—I dreamed of a day when I could walk into an Abercrombie & Fitch and buy a polo with the little moose insignia over the breast. Reading the catalogs, I fantasized about lying between the brawny chests of the Carlson twins. They had short brown hair and square jaws. To me they looked like gods, so masculine and strong. From the page, they stared at me the way I stared at Damon, the way my mom stared at the people on *Antiques Roadshow*. Rapt, like a spell had been cast.

That fall, I heard ads on the radio. A modeling agency was coming to Wichita, a forty-minute drive from Andale. Two girls from my school who had gotten a few gigs modeling for catalogs out of Wichita asked me if I'd heard about the international agency that was scouting through the Midwest. "Colton, how tall are your parents?" one of them asked.

"My parents?" I said. "My whole family is vertically challenged. I'm not tall enough to be a model." It was true: I was only five foot seven. But in a photograph, you couldn't tell exactly how tall someone was. Kate Moss, who I idolized from seeing her ads for Calvin Klein, was only five foot seven. I could be in a photo with her one day, right? I read about her exploits in the tabloids I leafed through at my friends' houses. She had a drink in one hand and a vial of coke in the other. She was wild, like my mom. I cut out her pictures and taped them to my wall. I wanted to be like her: idolized, desired. But I knew I couldn't do that in Kansas. Maybe this modeling agency was the first step.

"How does it work?" I asked.

"It's at this fancy hotel in Wichita," she said. "You know, by the RiverWalk? You go super early on a Saturday and wait in this long line, and these guys in suits and big sunglasses walk up and down and pull you out of line and then you have to *walk* for them in front of everyone. If you pass the test, they take you inside to meet with the panel of agents to see if you're, like, photogenic enough."

"So they're actually taking my picture?" I said. "It's not just about how tall you are? How much does it cost?"

"I think it's, like, $400?" she said. "But totally worth it. And you'll definitely get pulled out of line, because you'll be, like, the only guy. Plus, you'll get a full photo shoot out of it to start building your portfolio."

Four hundred dollars wasn't a lot of money to these girls, but it was to me. I didn't ask my mom for much, and I knew she was nervous about what the future held for me. Clinton was smart and ambitious; we actually thought he might go to college. My dreams were delusional. I wanted to be a member of NSYNC. I wanted men to drool when I walked into a room. I wanted to be a star, although for doing what, I couldn't say, since I had no discernible talent. I thought this could be the first step toward something. It was an investment in my future.

When my mom came home from the bar that night, I had my pitch ready. It would be my birthday present and my Christmas present. "We can't afford it, Lou Lou," she said.

"I never ask you for anything!" I said. "This is the only thing I've ever wanted! It's such a big opportunity!"

"I just don't have the money, baby," she said.

"Fine," I said. "I'm going to kill myself. Is that what you want?"

She gave me a long, hard look, like she was chewing it over. "God damn it, Colton," she said. "I'm going to have to get the money from Joe. You know that, right?" Joe was a local guy who drank to blackout at the bar every day, and my mom functioned as his primary enabler and chauffeur after he split his head countless times on the pavement outside the Little Bear. He helped her out with money sometimes in return for her companionship. Her beauty was her currency, and I wanted her to spend it on me.

We stared each other down, like gazing into a mirror, seeing who would break first.

She did. "Fine," she said. "What day is it? I'll take off work."

On Saturday morning, after she and I had fought over the bathroom mirror, we loaded up the Celica, bound for Wichita. I was wearing camouflage cargo pants, but I'd cut a notch into the hem with kitchen scissors so they would flare out, like the boot-cut pants everyone in the catalogs was wearing, and a yellow long-sleeved Abercrombie shirt—the only one I owned—that Meadow had sent me from Florida as a gift. The finishing touch was a puka shell necklace. My mom was wearing black slacks from her previous life as a banquet manager, a billowing white top, and chunky jewelry, a wad of Clorets mint gum in her mouth. She was furious about it, but she'd still dressed the part; she looked like a stage mom. In the car, she muttered under her breath, "Can barely keep our lights on, but spending all this money so the kid can be a model?" She shook her head, like she couldn't believe it.

"*You* were a model, out in California," I said, trying to point out her hypocrisy.

"I got paid for it, Lou Lou," she said. "Catalogs paid good money back then. Before having children ruined my body." I knew this was a creative reading of her career. An advertisement she'd appeared in had ended up in *Playboy*, but listening to her talk about her former days as a model, you'd think she'd been a centerfold.

At the hotel, the line wrapped all the way to the parking lot. I'd expected the hopefuls to be glamorous, coiffed, but the people there looked mostly ordinary—more like the people who we saw on *Antiques Roadshow* than the people who competed on *America's Next Top Model*. Their clothes were too tight, or unflattering. I hadn't realized there were this many people who also wanted to get out of Kansas.

We took our place in line. I was holding a bound photo album with flowers on it that my mom had gotten at the Dollar Tree. Inside were photos that I'd made Clinton take of me: One of me looking straight to camera, sullen. Another with my hair pulled back, smiling. Left and right profiles to show the structure of my jaw. Within minutes, I felt a tap on my shoulder. I turned to see a woman wearing glasses and a black skirt; she looked like a secretary, or a cult member. "You," she said. "Come with me." I turned excitedly to my mom. I knew this was it. I was so proud.

As predicted, there were no men in line; it was all girls. As I stomped past them, I could feel their eyes on me. I had been chosen. I was special. Next to me, my mom shook her head, like this was her worst nightmare, flinging her purse over her shoulder. *Here we go*.

In a conference room, I sat down in a folding chair between the other applicants; there were maybe twenty other people in there, and only one other man, who looked older, like his picture would be on the side of a Just For Men box. Finally, I was called up to stand in front of a panel of four judges: three women and one man. One of them gestured for me to hand them my book. They reviewed the photos, whispering back and forth, but I couldn't hear a word they were saying. Then they gestured to a photographer, who stepped forward and snapped a few Polaroids of me. I blinked at the flash.

"Is that your mom?" the man said to me. I nodded. He motioned her over. "Your son really has a shot at this," he murmured to her. It was all the encouragement I needed.

We bent over a printed-out contract, not reading any of the language, both eager to put our signatures on it. These were my agents now. I was officially a model.

Later that week was my first official photo shoot as a professional model. I'd been asked to bring a number of looks, so we spent all week driving from one thrift store to another, picking out garments we thought would photograph well. The photo shoot was thirty minutes, shot by a creepy guy with a disposable camera, who gave it to us afterward to develop the film.

I never heard from the agency again. If I'd had the foresight to look up this supposed international modeling agency, it would have been easy for me to see it was a scam, and not a particularly good one at that. These fake modeling agencies went from city to city, luring gullible Midwesterners into signing away sums of money for professional photo shoots that never led to any bigger opportunities. And yet, I was proud of those photographs. They captured the happiness I felt in that moment: the pride I took in being recognized for something. Bolstered by that new confidence, I believed I could finally go after what I wanted in life. And what I wanted was Damon.

Walking down the hallways of Andale High with a new swagger in my step, I carefully placed one of the photographs facedown right outside the doorway to the afterschool office, where Damon had a desk, so he'd think that I had dropped it on accident. Maybe he would ask what it was from, or maybe he would just see my beauty, the same beauty that had earned me this opportunity in the first place. I wanted him to feel about me the way I felt when I looked at models on film. Maybe he saw right through it. Or maybe he never found the picture at all.

⸻

I had the bug now. I knew I was destined for something more than this town, for more than washing dishes at the Little Bear for five dollars an hour. I wanted to live in a place where the streets were paved. Was that so much to ask?

Joe had given my mom an old computer, and I would boot it up in the afternoon after school, waiting through the squeal of the dial-up modem so I could study the world of modeling. There was Kate Moss, of course—she was already my icon—but there were so many others too: Adriana Lima, who looked like a baby in Polaroids but when she stepped before a camera, oozed sexuality. Sasha Pivovarova, looking icy on the cover of Italian

Vogue wearing a leather glove, her hand placed just so. Gemma Ward, whose doll-like features came to life when she walked a runway. Carmen Kass, with her handsome face, looking almost maternal—like she would take care of the younger models she met backstage at Fashion Week. Catherine McNeil, who was the bad girl of couture, and according to the message boards I was reading was sleeping with Freja Beha, the androgynous muse of Karl Lagerfeld.

And the photographers who shot these models were even better. I had seen Bruce Weber's work in the Abercrombie & Fitch catalogs I pored over, but there was more to photography than those all-American studs with muscled torsos and cheesy smiles. Steven Klein's photographs captured a grungy East London cool, patent leather and cigarettes. He made any model he shot sexy, like fashion porn—not a hint of innocence. Steven Meisel made models look like they were coated in wax: Their bodies gleamed, not a pore in sight. David LaChapelle made colorful, pop-art homoerotic fantasies. Everything was a scene. The model wasn't the only subject. Each detail helped tell the story; looking at the photo was like watching a movie in a single still.

The sight of certain photographs could bring me to tears. A black-and-white photograph of Kate Moss by Mario Testino, where her left eye is bruised as if she's been punched in the face, made me weep, maybe because it reminded me of my mom. Kate was so popular because she was a chameleon. She could look like a hundred different people. She could communicate a hundred different feelings with her eyes. It didn't matter that she was shorter than the other models. She was special.

The only thing keeping me from ascending to join their ranks was my modeling agent, who wasn't calling, because the entire thing was a scam, although I didn't know that at the time. But my delusions of grandeur were powerful enough that I was willing to set my sights on another way to leverage my looks: acting. This was something my mom had actually encouraged me to do; she'd thought I had a nice singing voice, which I could put to use in musical theater. Convincing her to drive me to theater tryouts in Wichita was less of a challenge than the modeling had been. She was the one who'd seen the ad in the newspaper.

Auditions for West Side Story were being held at a warehouse in Wichita. The production was being staged by a prestigious local youth theater program that funneled into a professional track. Unlike the modeling casting call, the kids gathered there looked like stars, like they'd come out of a Disney Channel factory. Competition was in the air. All of them could dance, act, and sing. I felt like a fool in my Pepto-pink button-up tucked into a pair of dark jeans, and my belt with its big brass buckle. The queen bee was a beautiful boy named Mo who was the best dancer of them all: He was already six foot two, with long, lean legs. His body wasn't flawlessly athletic, but he was so strong— the way he sashayed into a room was so balletic, like the score from Fosse was playing somewhere and only he could hear it. He moved like a wildcat. I was intimidated by him. I was intimidated by all of them.

We auditioned over the course of the weekend, and ultimately, I booked the role of Chino, with two speaking lines. Knowing that I would get to stand onstage with a theater full of people watching felt rapturous. As we were walking out of the theater, Mo glanced at me. "You gonna be at Shawna's house this weekend? She's having a party," he said.

"I don't know," I stammered.

"You should come," he said. "We hang there every weekend. It's hella fun."

I nodded. That would be nearly an hour away from Andale; there was no chance of my mom driving me there. "Maybe next weekend," I said.

"No worries." He shrugged. As he walked past me, he turned and called back: "Welcome to the group!" It was the first time I could remember genuinely belonging somewhere without having to monitor every detail about the way I presented myself to the world.

Back at school, with the renewed confidence that came with being an international top model and stage star, I set my sights back on Damon. He was working with the civics club, so I joined in order to get closer to him. It gave me something to do after school, and it was off-season for track, anyway. In the club meetings, I daydreamed about riding in his car, the way his muscular arm would feel hooked around my neck, the road ahead gleaming off his sunglasses. He was taciturn, but he was kind to me; at times it even felt like he was more interested in me than in the other kids, maybe because he knew how unreliable my mom could be. Even though we lived only a few blocks away from the school, she would often be late to come pick me up to take me to theater rehearsal in Wichita, or just not come at all. Finally, one day, he offered to drive me to rehearsal.

"Are you sure it isn't out of your way?" I said, feigning concern for inconveniencing him, even though this was exactly what I wanted. I lifted up my shirt to scratch the side of my abdomen, without breaking eye contact, in a gesture that I thought would look absentminded, even though it was all completely calculated.

"Nah," he said. "It's easy. You ain't afraid of dogs, are you?"

"I'm not afraid of much," I said. He gave me a funny look, like he knew I was trouble, which I was. On the way to his house, he turned his police siren on, and I watched as, like magic, traffic parted on the freeway to make space for us.

At home, my pivot to stardom wasn't going over well with my brother Clinton. He had always gamely ceded the spotlight to me in the car when we were kids and I would insist on playing the music I liked, but high school was a different playing field, and resentment began to build. He'd been happy in his first year at high school—he'd run track, starred in the school play, and gone to parties and football games. But when I arrived a year later, I was desperate for everyone to like me. I sucked all the air out of every room I was in, redirecting all attention toward myself, and away from him. All those cases of beer I'd stolen from the walk-in fridge to leave for the upperclassmen meant they knew me already; I could feel Clinton watching me from across the cafeteria, chewing on crinkle-cut French fries in a greasy paper basket, wondering how I was already better friends with them than he was. I signed up for extracurriculars—drama, choir, track—and he pulled out of them just as quickly.

He'd been using my mom's car to drive us to school; I arrived back at the car one day to find that it was gone. He'd left without me. I was furious. On the short walk home, I plotted the things I would tell my mom about how Clinton had abandoned me. But when I arrived, she was sitting at the kitchen table, crying.

"What's wrong?" I asked.

"Why do you need to hurt him this way?" she said.

"I don't know what you're talking about," I said. "He's such a fucking baby." But I knew exactly what she meant. It wasn't just that I wanted to shine on my own. I didn't want Clinton's shadow anywhere near me.

We'd become fiercely competitive, or maybe I was competitive with him, and he was just full of rage at why it seemed I was inexplicably trying so hard to obliterate him. We fought over bathroom time, who had the food stamp card, who drank the last of the milk, who got to use the computer. We broke each other's most beloved possessions, read each other's journals, spread rumors about one another in school. But we still shared a bedroom.

He started getting into increasingly worse trouble— dressing like a skater, smoking weed, drinking with his friends. When Clinton drank, he had the worst temper, just like my dad. What I couldn't see at the time was that we were recreating my parents' dynamic: I was my mother, manipulating him, egging him on, pushing him to the edge for reasons I didn't even understand, and he was my father, flying back in anger, which would allow me to play the victim, even though his reaction was exactly what I wanted.

I didn't think that he cared enough to check the search history on our computer, so I hadn't thought to delete it after I had been looking up "police porn." But then the door to our bedroom burst open, and Clinton had me pinned down on the bed and his fists were in my face. "What the fuck do you think you're doing, faggot?" he yelled.

I was sobbing. "You always call me a faggot," I said. "You always call me gay. I just wanted to see if I was." We never spoke about that again.

This was the pattern: I would meet Damon after school and ride with him back to Wichita, where I would wait at his house, which was about fifteen minutes outside town, for Mo to pick me up and take me to theater practice. Under other circumstances, maybe it would have raised eyebrows, but my family was notorious; everyone knew my mom was unreliable, and the fact that a man, in a position of authority, in a uniform no less, was taking any interest in me must have looked like a good thing. On my long drives with Damon to Wichita, we'd talk about our lives. He told me about his mother, and we talked about whatever my mom's latest misadventures were, whichever new scrape or scuffle she'd gotten herself into, and we talked about Clinton, who was acting out. "I feel like it's my fault," I said. "When I was in middle school and Clinton was a freshman, he'd been Manolo in the female version of *The Odd Couple*. That's a big part. Then when I get to Andale High, I get the lead. Over Clinton." I wanted to make myself the hero of the story—that my undeniable talent and charisma were wreaking havoc in my family, as opposed to the truth, which was that I was jealous of my brother. He had such a positive approach to everything; he saw the good in everything and everyone. When we were little, I had wanted to protect him from how cruel the world could be; now I wanted to physically snap him out of it so he could wake up to the reality of our situation: We were on food stamps. We got free lunches from school. Our mom was drunk, every day. I wanted to make him see that the grass wasn't always greener when we lived in the middle of a gravel parking lot. If I had to destroy him to make that happen, so be it.

"If you can just make it a couple more years, you'll be able to get out of this town," Damon said. "You're going to go far, I just know it." I looked at him sideways. I wondered why he didn't leave Kansas. But mostly I was grateful that he saw me as special.

One afternoon, Damon had driven me back to his house to wait for Mo to take me to rehearsal. He was walking through the laundry room to the garage, where his car was parked. "You and Mo better stay out of trouble downtown. Have a good rehearsal," he said. I could hear the sound of his voice and the sound of his boots on the floor. I don't know why that day I was finally brave enough, but I was. I had been waiting so long to say it, and we were alone, and I was finally ready.

"You don't have to leave," I said. I heard him stop. But I knew, I could feel, that he was panting. I was sure he wanted it too. And suddenly, I was in control, in a way I never had been before, where I could feel his desire for me even if I couldn't see it written across his face, and I knew that I had him.

"Come here," he said. I walked into the laundry room. He stood there. I thought he would be shaking from nerves, but he wasn't. "Get on your knees," he said.

After it was over, he threw a towel at me to clean myself up and jumped into the shower. I thought we'd lie together for a while; it was my first time going all the way, although he didn't know that. I stared up at the popcorn ceiling, the fan slowly oscillating. It was still daylight. His cum was inside me. I was fourteen. He was forty-two. The hot water was running distantly in the other room.

I thought once I'd had him, I would be satisfied. But I wasn't.

I wanted more.

5

WICHITA, KANSAS
2003

Because I knew you, I have been changed . . . for good!" Mo and I sang those lyrics as we sped down the I-21 freeway in his maroon Chevrolet Monte Carlo, the soundtrack to *Wicked* in an old Discman playing through an adapter plugged into the cassette deck on his stereo. It was our duet; we were soul mates, one another's missing piece, cut from the same cloth. I never would have thought that the diva of the theater, the performer who everyone idolized, would have become my best friend. It helped that I could be fully myself with him, in a way that I couldn't be anywhere else: I was still in the closet with nearly everyone except Damon, who was so much older than me that I didn't really see him as a peer. But with Mo, I felt no danger.

One day after rehearsal, we were stretching on the pavement in a vacant parking lot outside the convention center, all of us misfits with our legs extended atop parking meters, wearing leg warmers, drinking coffee and smoking cigarettes, binders full of sheet music and covered in Polaroids we'd taken of our adventures together. It was very *A Chorus Line*, if I'd known that reference at the time, which I didn't. But out the corner of my eye, I noticed a group of older actors—they looked to be in their twenties—walking out of the stage door across the parking lot.

"Who the fuck are they?" I asked. Were they holding auditions for a show? Why hadn't I been made aware of it?

"That's the summer stock company," Mo said. "The *professional* actors. They come from all over just to audition." He took a pull from his cigarette. "Those are the people we've spent all this time training to be. Those chorus boys get two hundred and fifty dollars a week—more if you're good enough to get an actual role." He stubbed it out. "That's the closest to Broadway any of us are likely to get."

Lust fell over me, like tunnel vision, as I watched the chorus boys saunter out of the stage door. They had statuesque dancer builds, implausibly huge bulges inside their cutoff jean shorts. They cantered like prizewinning dressage horses in brown leather flip-flops. Was I in heat?

Mo saw me looking at them. "Colton, why does everything always have to be about sex with you?" he said.

"Colton's always got dick on the brain," somebody else said, and we all laughed. It was true. I was fourteen years old and I thought about sex more than I thought about fried chicken, which was saying something, even though the only person I'd actually had sex with was Damon.

The adult theater production would occasionally let in students from the youth program. We had to try out, and maybe, I thought, then I could seduce one of those chorus boys.

The audition was what I'd come to expect from the world of theater: a panel of queens, looking at me in judgmental silence. Their eyes flickering over my shoes, then making sustained, painful eye contact with me. "Talk less," I imagined them saying as I stood there, stupidly. "Smile more." But, incredibly, after a lengthy audition process, Mo and I both booked parts—him as a lead chorus boy, which came as no surprise, since his dancing ability put the rest of us hopefuls to shame, and me as "Villager #2" in *Beauty and the Beast*, and an orchestra pit singer for the remaining shows that season. I was elated. Villager Number Two! It was the role I was born to play.

As Mo and I glided past the dressing rooms to the left of the mezzanine, I pulled my favorite trick and accidentally-on-purpose dropped a few headshots in the hopes that the chorus boys would stumble upon them. "There really isn't a line you wouldn't cross, is there?" Mo said.

"Is that an invitation?" I said, kissing him on one cheek as I said goodbye.

Sitting behind the steering wheel of the car my mom's new boyfriend had let me borrow—never mind that I only had a learner's permit, and was supposed to have a parent with me when I drove—I realized how good it felt to have a life that was bigger than Andale. Summer stock was underway and even though Mo's schedule was packed, because he was in every show, it felt like there was so much time. Our band of rebellious theater kids would meet up at the Wendy's for ninety-nine-cent junior bacon cheeseburgers with extra ranch, fries, and a large chocolate Frosty, when the machine wasn't broken. We chain-smoked menthols. We dreamed. Every day felt more exciting. Finally, I was a part of something where I could be completely myself.

I would wait for Mo under the old marquee in front of the theater, the one that still flickered even though it hadn't been in use for some time now. It was quiet in the city. You could hear the buzzing of the streetlamps. The electrical wires that ran from post to post made the performance hall feel like a circus tent—all of us kids readying our next act, before we packed up and headed on to the next city.

As Mo stepped out through the stage door, flanked by a few of the older girls, he looked at me and grinned. "Whole company's going out tonight," he said. "Buckle up, bitch."

"You have a fake ID, right?" one of the girls said.

I shook my head no. "Are they super strict?"

"I'm sure they'll let you in, Colton," Mo said. "You're the golden boy in training."

The bar was a short drive from the theater, but it felt like another world. Nobody was checking IDs at the door, so we made our way inside. The floors were glossed concrete, which gave the unsettling impression that a drink had been spilled at all times. There were neon-green strobe lights overhead, and purple-hazed ones behind the bar. Wet bar napkins stuck to the faded blacktop tables. One bathroom with a gender sign that just said: GAY. Cheap booze. Three old wooden boxes where the go-go boys would dance, by the DJ booth, which was really just a computer hooked up to multiple ten-inch subwoofers. A glory-hole scene from a leather porno could have been shot there at any time. It was grungy. It was dirty. I loved it.

Under the strobe light, two men were grinding on each other. I watched them—staring, actually, in what was probably an unguarded way—when I felt a tap on my shoulder. It was a manager, asking to see my ID. *Shit*. Mo's fake had cost him $150. I was gonna have to get creative.

As I was gently escorted out, I turned to see the name of the bar on the door. It was funny—I hadn't even noticed it. The bar was called Big Daddy's.

Outside of theater, life was insufferably boring. We'd said goodbye to the apartment on Main Street and moved out to a creaky old farmhouse with white chipped paint all over the siding and the faint, musty smell of cigarette smoke. Out my window was a huge front yard overgrown with weeds, and to the left was a dilapidated chicken coop with no chickens in it. It was an upgrade from the apartment; for this place, my mom was paying $750 a month. Upstairs, there were two bedrooms, one for me and one for Clinton. Next to our bedrooms was an A-frame attic that we converted to a bedroom for my aunt Cassie. My room was just big enough to fit a twin bed, a chair, and a fan. It was too hot, and I hated making my bed, so I never used blankets or sheets. I just slept on the mattress, on a box spring on the floor.

There was nothing on the walls, but I wanted it that way: clean, simple, easy to leave. In the apartment, I'd papered the walls of my room with photos: Christina Aguilera and Jolene Blalock from *Maxim*. Anna Kournikova and Jessica Alba from *FHM*. Obviously, I didn't want to fuck those girls; instead, I wanted to have the freedom to express femininity the way they did. I had grown ever more obsessed with celebrities, obsessed with the prospect of being a star. I sent tapes to Rosie O'Donnell of myself doing choreography to NSYNC, praying that she would respond. I'd call into the radio station so I could win a Tori Amos CD and a free Papa John's pizza. I had to call in every single night, even during my birthday party. The computer had broken, and I didn't have a cell phone, so there really was nothing to do, which may have been a blessing in disguise: It was easier, then, to drive cars around fields and jump into ditches, to do whatever you wanted with no consequences.

This new house was nicer, but it was still a dump. And God, it was hot. There was always dust and cobwebs. You could hear the wind whistling through the window—not howling, but singing. The paint would turn yellow from the cigarette smoke. There was never silence, because Donovan or Prince or the Stones were always playing from my mom's old boom box with the cassette player, the one that she'd had forever. I'd lie on that mattress looking up at the ceiling, dreaming of getting out of Kansas. Dreaming of a life that didn't feel like this one.

Eventually my dad had moved to Kansas, one final chess move in the long game he and my mom had been playing my whole life. He'd gotten a job managing a security self-storage in Wichita, and he brought Margaret along with him. Clinton and I would go visit them in their one-bedroom apartment, right behind the office of the storage facility, behind a Sonic—if you managed the place, you had to live on the premises.

Dad had calmed down as he'd gotten older, or maybe he was exhausted in a way that I interpreted as calm. Eventually he admitted that the exhaustion was from throat cancer, but you couldn't tell

he was sick until after he'd gotten a tracheotomy, and had to hold
a little device to his sunspotted neck to speak. His voice sounded
gravelly and robotic, but also kinder than it used to. It was as if, in
his sickness, he'd realized that he should be better to people, and
that he didn't have to be so angry all the time. We'd walk through
the front office and wave to Margaret, who would be busy helping
customers, and find my dad on the golf cart, surveying the units,
chewing on Skoal, which had come to replace his Marlboro Reds.
He'd have a white Styrofoam spit-cup in one hand, his jug of sweet
tea in the other. He looked exactly like Burt Reynolds, and he knew
it. Afterward, we'd retire to the apartment, where he'd sit in his
used brown recliner watching shows about cars. He wanted an
old Dodge Charger, or an old Camaro; I dreamed of driving a '69
Corvette Stingray.

He had lost his teeth and was wearing dentures now; he used
to pop them in and out of his mouth to make us laugh. He was
still ruddy in the face, and his hair had gone white. He wore a
uniform of baggy jeans, dirty white sneakers, a white undershirt,
and a flannel. His refrigerator never had anything in it, and his
shirt was always stained with tea. But he was so content—like he
couldn't ask for anything more out of life. Part of it was that he'd
found God. He would invite us to come to church with him in a
neighboring town. Clinton wanted to go so he could spend time
with our dad, but I only went because it was next to an Arby's and
a Dairy Queen. We sat in the pew singing: *"This is a church on fire
/ This is the Holy Spirit flame / We have a burning desire / To lift up
Jesus' name."* I didn't believe in any of it, but I liked the theater of
it—the drama.

And yet he was still the same in so many ways. He moved
through a room as if he were the only one in it; he didn't see any

of us. He was so used to people doing everything for him that he'd forgotten how to do anything for others. Clinton still looked at him like he was a superhero, and I couldn't understand why. I sniped at him about it when we came home from church. "Are you blind?" I said. "What has he ever done for you besides make Mom's life miserable? You look at him like he's your idol and it's fucking pathetic."

"He's our blood," Clinton said.

I wanted to ask my father why he didn't fight for my mom instead of fighting with her, why he didn't see her as a prize instead of as a punching bag. But I never asked. I just sat on the floor while *Motor Trend* played on the grainy television, while he lay in his recliner, spitting chew into a Styrofoam cup.

If you had asked me at the time, I would have told you that I didn't care about getting my father's attention. Why would I want his when I could have Damon's? He would still pick me up in Andale and take me back to his house and I would blow him in the laundry room, or he would fuck me in the bathroom, my hands gripping the tile ridge of the tub, or he would handcuff me to the metal bed frame. I wanted it, not only because I was a hormonal teenager but also because I wanted him to love me the way I loved him, and I imagined that if I did those things it would make him love me and see me as an adult rather than as the child that I was.

But Damon was edgy during sex—like he wanted to get it over with, or like he wasn't enjoying it the way I wanted him to. Every time felt like it might be our last. I lived in a state of constant dread that he would turn to me after it was over, undone by shame, and

say, "I don't think we should do this anymore." It was as if I already
knew that this was how people would come to see me—as disposable, like trash, something you could discard once you were finished with it.

So when he asked whether I wanted to come to an overnight
fellowship retreat where he would be a chaperone, I thought it
might be a chance to have something more like an adult getaway.
I'd never been to anything like that before; we couldn't afford things
like that. But Damon offered to pay for me.

I fantasized about it for weeks. I planned my outfits. I envi-
sioned Damon picking me up in the long dirt driveway that led
up to the farmhouse, my mom looking out the window and seeing
him, this man picking me up to take me away for the weekend,
and something crossing her face—jealousy, even rage—as she
watched me get into the passenger seat of his car. The men she
brought home rarely had cars; they were like strays. But here I
was, all of fourteen, able to pull a man, a real man, with authority. Then he and I would get to know each other even better on
the long drive, in the intimate space of his cop car, that protected
little world, locked behind the metal doors and glass windows that
beaded sunshine across my face. We would drive in the woods,
past long, dark vast expanses of trees you could see for miles
through the mountains. We'd be laughing and singing along to
songs that we both loved on the radio, the wind enveloping me,
drawing me closer to him, into his arms, under the overpasses on
the highway, bathed in the neon light of a truck stop or a vacant
motel. I was delusional. But they were my delusions, and I loved
them.

Reality set in as soon as I boarded a dingy yellow school bus
with the other teens. They were sweaty and pimpled, braces

webbed with rubber bands, draining Capri-Suns through those teeny-tiny straws, the smell of Lunchables wafting through the heat, whispering secrets from row to row and playing with hand-made cootie-catchers. I wanted to jump out the window. This was how Damon saw me. I sat there the whole drive, thinking about how furious I would be with Damon when I told him that he had abandoned me, stuck me with those children. I was not a child.

It didn't look like I'd imagined. I found my bunk in a little log cabin, a tiny room with three bunk beds, which I was shar-ing with kids I didn't know. Discovering this, that I'd have no privacy, only infuriated me more. Within minutes of arriving, the door creaked open and Damon entered. I heard him first—he stomped the way all officers do when they enter a room, like everyone needs to acknowledge their presence—but when I turned to face him, he was wearing civilian clothes. It was the first time I'd seen him in public without his uniform. I had seen him in other ways—wearing gym shorts in his house, or with them around his ankles while I was on my knees, and I had seen and felt what seemed like every part of his body all over me and inside me, but it was different, seeing him in this context. His blue eyes stood out even more now that they weren't blending in with his police uniform. He was wearing cargo shorts and a pastel T-shirt, like the flesh of a blood orange, and it turned my anger to lust.

"Hello there, Officer," I said in my best horny cheerleader voice.

"Hello, Mr. Haynes," he said in a similar intonation. To the other kids in the room, it would have sounded like he was mock-ing me, but I knew what he was doing. It was our secret language.

"Can you help me bring the firewood over tonight from the main lodge?"

"Of course I can, sir. Need help with anything else?" I said, trying not to smile.

I showered in what looked like an outhouse, with a bar of soap attached to the wall by a thick white rope. Then I met Damon at his car so we could drive up to the main lodge. He parked behind a shipping container, leaned over, and started kissing me. His gun was in its holster in the center console. Then we were in the back seat, then my knees were in the dirt. I was up against the back trunk of the car. My face pressed against the glass, my hands where he could see them.

His hands gripped my brown hair, curled at the end, almost hard enough to let me know that if I tried to leave, there would be consequences. But I wanted him to pull harder. I wanted him to yank the hair out of the back of my head so I could have a bald spot as a reminder of what he did to me forever.

After he came, he zipped his fly up without saying a word while I fumbled with my pants, now dirty around my ankles.

"Do you think they can see us?" I said.

Damon flinched. "Who?" he said. "Is somebody coming?"

I looked up. "The stars," I said. I thought it would sound romantic. But he just looked at me as if I were an alien, or a little kid.

In the morning my handprints were all over the car like evidence. I kept waiting for somebody to notice, but nobody did.

I was convinced that Damon's interest in me was dwindling. Maybe mine was in him too. It was summer, and I was seeing him less, and seeing more of my new friends from the theater program, who weren't gay in the way Damon was gay—a cop, steeped in masculinity—but gay in a way that felt celebratory, free. That was exciting to me. It was something I hadn't experienced before. Damon told me what to do in a manner that was almost paternalistic. Even then, I was self-aware enough to be reminded of my father.

What I wanted was to hang out in places like Big Daddy's— where men congregated, where I could be the center of attention, where I could be desired. And I'd concocted a plan for how I was going to get in. I had my eye on a company boy named Ben. He was twenty-one, and his affect, like Damon's, was all machismo—he wanted to talk about sports, cars, and which girls I had my eye on, which had to be bluster, because surely he knew I was gay—but I'd heard rumors that he was bisexual. After one long day of tech rehearsals, I spotted Ben sitting alone at the base of the piano, removing his battered Capezios. I made up an excuse about not being able to go home to Andale before I was meeting up with friends that evening, and asked if I could shower at his place; I knew he lived nearby.

Now I wonder what he thought of this—the way he saw me. Fourteen years old, with a cherub's face and swoopy Disney star hair—did he know what I was up to? Either way, he said yes. Back at his place, I gave him a blow job, and when he got in the shower, I knew this was my opportunity. Naked, I crept out of his bed and rummaged through his jeans, which were still crumpled on the floor, until I found his dark leather billfold. I opened it up, and there was his ID. We looked just enough alike that it might work. *Jackpot.* This would be my ticket into Big Daddy's.

I left his apartment feeling triumphant—like I had actually accomplished something that was going to benefit me going forward. I would finally get to be around the older boys, and I could make more money working at the gay bar than I could washing dishes at the Little Bear. I was going to be a go-go boy.

Walking back into Big Daddy's, I saw the same manager who had escorted me out weeks earlier. I felt confident, even cocky; he must have seen the chaos in my eyes.

"Hi. I'm Ben," I said. "I wanna dance here."

He once-overed me. He smirked. "Okay, Ben," he said. "How old are you?"

"Twenty-one," I said. I pulled out the ID and he studied it. He must have seen that our faces didn't match, but did it really matter?

"We don't have dancers on payroll," he said. "But they work for tips on the weekend. Under the table only."

"I can do that," I said.

"Don't ask questions," he said. "Don't answer questions. Don't drink on the job. And don't tell anyone your real name." He looked down at the ID. "Your name is Ben. Got it?"

I nodded.

"See you Friday at eight," he said.

Dancing was exhilarating. The thumping of the beat rattled the club like a cage, and from up there on the box, all the men looked like wild animals. The music was so loud, it felt like being inside someone's heart, like the bass itself was a heartbeat. We danced in cowboy hats and low-rise boot-cut jeans, sweat trickling down our abdomens toward our crotches, which were always shaved, no underwear. An elastic band would be wrapped around one of our biceps, or one of our thighs if we were wearing cutoffs, for the men to slip cash into. You could see our power. The cash on our bodies said it all: If you want a taste, empty your wallet. It wasn't about being a good dancer—it was about being eye candy.

Mo and I would rummage through racks and racks of old clothes at the thrift store, looking for things we could wear. He loved to forage for dancewear, and every so often he'd find the holy grail—a mesh tank, particularly a tight black crop that hit just above his navel. I hoarded camouflage cargo pants from the military thrift store, which I thought looked particularly stylish with a neon tank and a bucket hat. Sometimes I wore motorcycle gloves, with a shiny metal button on each side. Nothing ever matched. Our clothes looked like costumes that a boy band would wear in a music video, only sluttier. *Slut* was the mood I was after at all times. If someone called me a slut, I thanked them and took it as a compliment. I wanted to gag them with my beauty. I wanted them to gag over me.

I was using the way I looked the way my mom always had—not that she had any idea that I was doing this when I was out of the house. To her, it would have affirmed a fear that I was just like her in the deepest ways. Turning a blind eye to my behavior meant she didn't have to look in the mirror and reckon with how she might have helped steer me toward a more stable life if she'd been able to help herself first. But this—using my sexuality—all came so naturally to me: It was like it was in my blood.

On my third weekend dancing at Big Daddy's, I caught the eye of a guy who wasn't a daddy at all—he couldn't have been older than twenty-five, or much taller than five foot six. He had a beautiful, muscular body and he was wearing a cowboy hat. He motioned for me to get off the box after one number, and when I did, he placed the cowboy hat on my head and grabbed me by my waist, pulling me toward him. His name was Max, and he became the closest thing I'd had to a real boyfriend. He had a real job, working for AT&T, which meant that he had money—and that meant a car, a nice apartment, and freedom. I started spending the night at his place in Wichita.

Max wasn't at the bar the night Big Daddy's threw its annual White Party. I was wearing a pair of chalky Levi's, a wet see-through tank top, and an acid-washed cowboy hat. I had moved boxes into the middle of the club and was scanning the room through the technicolor neon lights, when out of the corner of my eye I caught a shimmer of blond from the top of a man's head. It was Damon. We locked eyes. His stare made my stomach drop. Quickly, he walked over to me, grabbed me by my wrist, and yanked me off the box. The club was so packed, no one even noticed. He was yelling at me, but the music was so loud I could barely hear him. "What the fuck are you doing here?" he was saying. "You can't be here. How do you even know about this place?"

I wrapped my arms around him as he pulled me to the back of the club, through a cloud of cigarette smoke. I didn't put up a fight. The vision of him, the smell of him, made me nostalgic for a past that felt so far away, even though it had only been a few months earlier when it felt like me and him against the world. I cried into his neck. "I'm sorry," I said, over and over again, "I'm sorry," and I let him carry me out.

The fact that I was sleeping with anyone who locked eyes with me—with Damon, with Max, with Ben, with other men I met at the club, with the older musical theater boys—wasn't lost on

Mo. Even though he was my best friend, sometimes he looked at me as if we were more than that, like he didn't understand why I lavished sexual attention on everyone but him. One night Mo and I were dancing at the club, all the men ogling us while we put on a show for them, laughing at the spectacle of it, oily, half-dressed, and too young to be in a place like that. When he kissed me, I kissed him back, not thinking much of it. He was my best friend, my lifeline; he felt more a part of me than my own family. It hadn't occurred to me that that kiss would change our relationship forever. When I pulled away from him, his eyes were bright, and full of expectation.

We exited the club holding hands, as we always did, and went back to his apartment, creeping slowly up the steps so we wouldn't wake his mom up. If she knew I had been crashing in his closet without her permission, we'd both be dead. In his bedroom, he sprawled out on the bed. His skin was glistening.

"Wanna be on top," he said softly. And he gave me that look, that look I'd seen from men so many times already, that look of *wanting*. I never knew how to say no to that look because I wanted so badly to be wanted, and so I did what I thought I needed to do. The second I felt myself enter him, I could feel our friendship rupturing, like suddenly we were miles apart even though I was inside him. Immediately I wanted to go back to where we'd been before, but it was too late.

Sex to me wasn't an expression of love. It was just a tool to get what I wanted. I had desired Damon, but I didn't love him the way I loved Mo, my friend, someone I desperately didn't want to hurt. I was painfully attracted to him, but I didn't know how to tell him that my love for him was different, too pure to contaminate with something as common as sex. And when he wanted that from me, it confirmed the thing that I already knew: It was all I was good for. It was the validation I had been chasing from everyone but him. I didn't know how not to do it. And as I came, I thought to myself, *You piece of shit.* I was ashamed that I'd let this happen.

Mo and I fucked all summer, mostly at his place, but one night he came to the farmhouse in Andale after giving in to one of my mom's countless invitations. She loved him too. It was hot, blisteringly hot, and the fan was so loud we knew nobody else in the house could hear the bed creaking. Sweat dripped from Mo's forehead onto mine. He was on top of me, his mouth tasting like coconut ChapStick, wearing a black do-rag, with a breathtaking pearly white smile. Once we finished, I was thirsty, so I went downstairs, the steps creaking under me, shifting my weight on the balls of my feet to try to minimize the noise. It was past midnight. My mom was at the table. There was an overhead light illuminating her. When she was drunk, she had this look like she had just been fucked, then dragged through a field. She looked tired and mean.

"What the fuck were you doing up there?" she said, slurring.

"What do you mean?" I said, starting to panic. This couldn't be happening. This wasn't what was supposed to be happening. I was meant to take this to my grave, or at least to someplace outside Kansas. "I'm just getting a glass of water."

"Tell me what the fuck you were doing," she said. There was a wicker basket on the table, and my mom's cigarette roller, and a bag of tobacco with rolling papers, and a handle of Northern Lights whiskey, which she drank because it was cheap and got her drunk fast. "I heard you. Tell me what you were doing."

"I don't know what you're talking about," I said. I started

to well up. I knew I was going to break. "We weren't doing anything." I could hear Mo's footsteps on the stairs, and I was praying he wouldn't come down. All my friends already knew my mom could be volatile, but not like this. "Fine," I said. "If what you're trying to get me to say is that I'm gay, then fine. I'm fucking gay."

"No, you're not," my mom said. "You're just doing this to hurt me."

I grabbed a plastic cup and filled it up with water from the tap. Mo was standing in the hallway. "Let's go," I said to him, and we went upstairs and I threw some clothes into a duffel bag, and I was crying, although I didn't know exactly why. Surely she had known already, I thought. She'd seen me dancing in her heels many times as a little boy, listened to countless hours of NSYNC on a loop while I practiced choreography in front of my mirror with her hairbrush, saw the way I lit up at the mention of anything musical theater, and caught me practicing my modeling faces, like Tyra told me to do. She'd seen scratch marks on my back from Damon and asked me where I'd gotten them; I had lied, of course, but she had to know the truth. Why was this such a big deal? Why did it matter?

When we came back downstairs, she was sobbing at the table.

"If you have such a problem with it, that's fine," I said. "You'll never have to deal with me again."

She stood up. "Don't you leave!" she yelled. "Don't you dare leave!"

I slammed the screen door, the noise of it bouncing off the frame and reverberating in the night. For miles on the road to Wichita, I heard it echoing in my mind, the sound of that one door shutting, the sound of something ending.

I couldn't bear to return home after that. I would crash at Damon's, which meant fucking Damon, and sleep at Max's, which meant fucking Max, and stay at Mo's, which meant fucking Mo, and then I would dance at Big Daddy's, which meant fucking the box, fucking the air, fucking the strobe lights, fucking the men who stuffed dollar bills in the rubber band around my thigh, and I wanted to be wanted but I wondered—why was it never enough? And why did all that wanting leave me feeling so empty?

For the rest of the summer, I spent most nights sleeping in Mo's closet, since we were in theater together, but once school started, I was back at Damon's. After school, he'd pull me into an empty office so I would give him head under his desk. I was in a fugue state. In class, I'd zone out, staring at the clock, waiting as the hands inched closer toward the sounding of the final bell when I'd be set free. The other kids at school were busy making weekend plans or studying for tests, but I was planning where I'd sleep that night, how I'd get there, and who I would have to manipulate to make that happen. My saving grace was that Max had bought me a cell phone because he was tired of trying to track me down—a black-and-silver Motorola flip phone. My mom hadn't formally kicked me out, but I didn't know how to go back to the farmhouse and see her after my disastrous coming-out.

One Thursday night, Max picked me up from working a private event at Big Daddy's that felt too lucrative to miss, and drove me back to his apartment. We were lying in bed when the cell phone rang—it was the farmhouse. I picked up and heard my brother's voice. "Colton," he said. "Come home."

"I told you not to call me this late," I said.

"Dad's dead," he said.

"Max and I are sleeping," I said, and hung up the phone.

"Who was that?" Max asked.

"Clinton," I said. "My dad died." When the words came out of my mouth, it sounded like it wasn't a big deal at all. As if he were nothing more than a goldfish. I felt nothing, like some self-protective survival instinct run amok.

"Oh my God," Max said. "Do you need me to take you home?"

"No," I said. I rested my head on his chest. "I'll only make things worse." I didn't feel sad. I didn't feel anything.

I skipped school the next day. Death made a great excuse. Clinton called me all weekend; I ignored all his calls. I went to rehearsal, danced at Big Daddy's with Mo, and crashed at Max's, as if everything were normal—as if the world hadn't changed overnight. Finally, on Sunday night, Max drove me out to Andale, back to the farmhouse. I gripped the car door the whole drive out, knowing that when I saw my mom and my brother, it would be real. Max said he would wait for me in his car down the road; he knew my family dynamic well enough to know that things could get heated quickly. And as soon as I walked through the front door, they did. "Colton!" my brother yelled. "Get the fuck in here."

In the kitchen, all my father's belongings were in piles on the floor. A military flag, an old suitcase. Trucker hats. Memorabilia that he'd been keeping in his apartment and in the security self-storage. Clinton was kneeling, his lip quivering. He looked like he'd slept there, clutching that military flag in his hands, like he hadn't left the room since they had retrieved the items days earlier. He was holding a photo. "This was the only thing on his fridge," he said.

He handed it to me and I looked down at the picture. The boy in the photo was wearing a forest-green cable-knit sweater with white stripes on the sleeves. His hair was freshly cut. He was grinning a big, plasticky smile, as stiff as the gel in his shellacked hair. It was me, taken the day of my eighth-grade graduation.

I looked over to my mom, who was sitting at the kitchen table. A cigarette smoldered between her fingertips, almost down to the filter, and there was a bottle of whiskey in front of her. They had both been waiting for me to come home, and the fact that I hadn't—the fact that I hadn't cared enough to do so—had come through loud and clear. "You really don't give a fuck, do you?" my mom said. "You really don't give a fuck that your father is dead."

I didn't say anything. I just rolled my eyes and started to walk upstairs, and she stood and grabbed the collar of my shirt. I cried out and tried to throw her off me, but she gripped harder. I turned to face her and she slapped me.

"Why couldn't you at least have some goddamn respect for me?" she said. "Why do you always want to hurt me? Why couldn't you do this for your brother? Why couldn't you be there for us?"

She slapped me again. A sea of raging emotion flooded through me as my vision began to blur from anger, and as I tried to pass her one more time, she clawed at my neck and wouldn't let go, so I shoved her against the table and ran out through the side door. I could still feel where her nails had dug into the back of my neck. My shoes slipped in the mud as I ran through the field. Finally, I kicked my shoes off and left them there, fumbling in my pocket for my phone to call Max to come and get me.

I found him on the main road a few minutes later. I was winded, and my neck was bleeding. As I got into Max's car, my feet muddy, I didn't have words to speak. Tears streamed down my face, silent ones, while I watched the lights flicker past us as we drove away.

"Hurry up!" Clinton said as I threaded my tie through its messy knot. "We're gonna be late!" It was odd to see him here, in Max's apartment, like a normalization of the fact that I was gay, or an acceptance of it. But the distance had been good: It had neutralized the competitive edge between us. Now he had come to Wichita to take me to our father's funeral; my mom was coming with Joe, and Clinton had borrowed her car to pick me up. "You're going to be okay, kiddo," Max said, and he kissed me on the cheek as Clinton and I left.

No sooner had we gotten on the road than I noticed red and blue lights flashing in the periphery. Cops. Of course we were being pulled over on the day of our father's funeral—why wouldn't we be? Of course we didn't have updated registration—we never did. Nobody in Andale did, to be fair, but we were in the big city of Wichita—small-town rules didn't apply.

As the police officer approached the driver's-side window, I heard my brother gulp in anxiety. A few tears dripped from his eyes. We were teenagers, but we must have looked like outlaws on the run. Maybe that's what we were—always running from instability and sadness, from broken homes and bruised egos, wishing we'd arrive at a destination that resembled normal, two bandits on the lam.

"Good morning, Officer," Clinton said.

"License and registration," the officer said, his eyes unreadable behind his aviator glasses.

"Officer," Clinton said, and he sniffled. "We're on our way to our dad's funeral."

The cop took his glasses off. "Are you lying to me, young man?" he said.

Clinton shook his head. "No, sir." More tears streamed down his face. The cop peered into the car at me. The funereal black of our cheap clothes must have been a giveaway.

"I'll let you off with a warning," he said. "Sorry for your loss. Mind your speed from now on." I hadn't even had to call Damon, who'd called sheriffs who had written me tickets and gotten them expunged before. This felt like the first lucky thing that had happened to me in forever.

At the entrance of the cemetery, we entered through a giant Gothic gate, then followed the signs that read William Clayton Haynes. Clinton was still crying. I still felt nothing. We rolled past the gravestones, through grand displays of love from families who could afford to show it, bouquets that rivaled those you might see on TV during the Rose Bowl parade. Finally, we arrived at a clearing near the east corner. We parked the car and walked up to the small crowd that was gathered around the casket. My dad had been cremated, but this, I figured, was standard procedure. There was no gravestone, and no flowers. It felt like we'd won a funeral giveaway from the radio—the bare-bones, minimum package.

There were about fifteen people gathered there; I only knew Margaret, Clinton, my mother, and Joe. As we took our seats in the front row, I felt oddly haunted, and a little angry, but not sad in the way I'd imagined I would feel. The funeral director started talking into a microphone, but I couldn't take in the words she was saying. And then—*bam!* Gunshots were fired and trumpets began to play. I'd forgotten my dad had served in the Army, which meant a gun salute would be standard. Something about the sound of "Taps" began tugging at my heartstrings, and I felt sadness brimming within me like a storm cloud threatening to dissolve into rain. I began to sob, bent over, with my head between my knees. You could have heard me from across the cemetery. And when I was done, I left my feelings there, like flowers on my father's gravesite.

What does it look like when a person unravels? I had never known, really, until I saw what my father's death did to my mother. She was hardly a model of stability in the first place, but things took a turn once he was gone. The light went out inside her. They had spent so many decades fighting and fucking and hating and loving one another. The loss, to her, was unimaginable. Later, I discovered that they had been planning to get back together; he had promised her that he was going to leave Margaret and reunite with her. Then, in the midst of that, he had taken a fatal dose of OxyContin and Lortab. He took so much that we all knew it had been suicide, although Margaret was still insisting that it was an accidental overdose so she could attempt to sue the prescribing doctor.

Every time I came home to the farmhouse, my mom was drunk, an empty eighteen-pack of Natty Light and another bottle of cheap whiskey on the table. The gas company kept turning off her service, so there was never any heat; after countless times cleaning myself with cold water in the sink, I resolved not to come back. The only reasons to visit were to see Clinton and to pick up my monthly check from Social Security, for $750, that we got after my dad died—a recurring benefit until we turned eighteen. After realizing that my mom was drinking the money away instead of paying the bills with it, Clinton and I began waiting by the mailbox on the days we knew the checks were likely to come, wrestling her for them. She looked pained when we made off with the unopened envelopes, triumphant. "God damn it," she yelled after us as we ran down the dirt road, "I'm going to have to go fuck Joe for $1,500!" It didn't faze me that my father was gone. He was just a man, and not a particularly important one to my story; when had he ever shown me that he loved me? A refrigerator photograph, swiftly cataloged, the resentment fresh in my mind.

Damon—now that was a story worth telling. That was a man who chose to love me, who loved me because he saw something in me worth loving. If I'd been forced to tell someone what was happening between us, I would have insisted that I seduced him. I was the aggressor. I wore him down. That's a feeling I still carry with me to this day. I wasn't a victim. He saw my worth. Did it matter that in the eyes of the law he was a predator who groomed me and took advantage of me? Such an idea would never have occurred to me then. I would have defended him until my last breath. He fucked me because he loved me. That's what a man did when you mattered—when you were valuable. Right? Or did men fuck you because you were worthless, as a way of giving you your value? Both things felt true. I wanted him to cuff me to the cage in his cop car so he could hold me hostage long enough for me to believe that this was what true love felt like.

Not long after my father died, I was in the civics club with Damon. Suddenly the principal was in the doorway. Damon stood and they spoke for a minute in hushed tones, then Damon turned and looked at me. "Colton," he said. "Can you speak with us in the hall for a minute?"

My mom had called me in to social services as a runaway. I had to go to a children's home in Wichita. "They're sending someone for you," the principal said.

"That's not necessary," Damon said. "I can take him there."

"You don't mind?" the principal said.

Damon shook his head. "Not one bit," he said.

I was shaking as I pulled my things from my locker. The inside of it was papered with photos of myself—the stupid modeling photos from the photographer I never heard from again, from the agent who had turned out to be a scam, and as I looked at them I couldn't believe how stupid I was. Stupid and good for only one thing.

In Damon's car, I watched as the little town of Andale flipped past us. Past the park that housed the memories of Summerfest and shaving cream fights, past the outdoor basketball court where I'd learned to shoot hoops. Past streets where I'd gotten into fistfights and stargazed. Past the dilapidated tennis court next to the town pool with a two-dollar entrance fee for locals, where I'd tasted peanut butter M&M's for the first time. Past the monkey bars where I'd staged gymnastic routines for anyone who would watch. Past the once-white water tower that now stood chipped, looking ready to burst, like me. Kids frolicking in the ditches, dancing down dead-end roads. This town.

"What's going to happen to me?" I asked Damon.

"Don't worry," Damon said. "We'll figure it out."

He took me to the drive-thru at McDonald's for a Happy Meal. I wondered what the girl at the window thought of us. Maybe she thought we were father and son.

I inhaled the burger and fries while he sailed along the highway, his arm around my shoulder, the sky an airless blue before us. I shook the empty bag. There was a toy at the bottom. I pretended to look at it as he drove. A melody rattled around in my head: *"Because I knew you, I have been changed . . . for good!"*

"You okay, baby?" he said. I nodded and looked out the window. The gold of his badge reflected off the windshield, like a diamond in the sunlight. I held the toy in my hand, this cheap plastic thing. It was cute, but I knew it was disposable. Something you played with until you were sick of it, then never thought about again.

I watched the cornfields roll past, wondering when he would let me go.

PART
TWO

6

NEW YORK CITY
2004

The plane touched down just after 8:00 p.m. and I jolted awake in my seat, fumbling with my backpack. As people shuffled down the aisle, all of them looking busy and important, like they had places to be, I stayed in my seat until a flight attendant approached.

"Unaccompanied minor?" she said.

I nodded.

"Follow me," she said.

A handler greeted me at the mouth of the jetway and walked me out of the airport, explaining exactly where to get a yellow cab so as not to get scammed by an unlicensed driver. I nodded, not really listening, and at baggage claim promptly got into a car with the first guy who approached me. Out the window, skyscrapers loomed in the distance. This was my home now. This was what I was meant to do. This was where I belonged.

"Canal and Lafayette, right?" the driver said.

"I think so," I said, unsure and extremely carsick.

"Eighty bucks," he said.

Shit. That was way more than this was supposed to cost. "Isn't it supposed to be forty?" I said.

"Eighty."

I counted out four twenties from the envelope of cash that I had saved up from my Social Security checks and lugged my two enormous suitcases out of the trunk, scanning the crowded streets for the address on the paper printout I had folded in my pocket. I'd never been to New York before—the biggest city I'd ever been to was Dallas. The sheer volume of people on the street was overwhelming. The smells of hot garbage wafted up from the gutters. It felt like you could feel steam rising off people. Deliverymen sailed down Canal on bicycles, darting between taxis. There were neon lights everywhere. It was dizzying.

I was a few blocks off. I wiped the perspiration on my forehead onto my tank top as I tugged my suitcases down the packed sidewalk. Finally, I found a door next to a Chinese restaurant with the right number on it and hit the buzzer.

A voice crackled back at me: "Hello?"

"Hi!" I said. "I think I live here?"

"Come on up," the voice said. Sweat dripped down my front as I clambered up three flights of stairs, painted red, just like the exterior of the Chinese restaurant below, slipping on the floor in my brown leather flip-flops. Standing at the top of the stairs, with the door open, was an implausibly handsome man. He had eyes set wide, deep in his perfectly symmetrical face. He looked like a cobra, ready to strike.

"Hey, bud," he said. He had a slight accent I couldn't place, but it sounded exotic. "I'm Eugene."

"Colton," I said. I shook his hand, holding myself up straight, trying to seem masculine and mature. He sized me up. I must have looked like a kid—six inches shorter than him, and only fifteen.

"Let me show you around," he said, and he led me inside, grabbing one of my suitcases by its handle and wheeling it into the hallway.

The apartment was as crowded as the street outside; it looked as if it had been subdivided, with walls where there shouldn't be walls. Beer bottles and trash were on every surface. Two men, both of them tall and chiseled like statues, sat on a cracked black leather couch chatting with two beautiful girls; with a start, I realized one of the girls had been the winner of *America's Next Top Model* the season before. They glanced at me as I walked past, and I felt suddenly small and childlike. They were so tall; they looked like runway models, probably because they were.

In one of the bedrooms, there was a pair of bunk beds made up with sheets, then a bare mattress on the floor. "Make yourself at home," Eugene said. I set my bags down by the mattress. I was starving, but there was nothing here for me to eat, I didn't want to spend the little money I had on food, and besides, I'd spent the whole summer trying to lose as much weight as possible so I'd look gaunt and angular in my Polaroids. I was the ninth tenant: There were eight other male models living in that apartment, all of them in their mid-twenties, all of them already working; some of them breezed in and out to introduce themselves, trailing clouds of Acqua di Giò and cigarette smoke. None of them were wearing shirts. *Where were their shirts?*

"We're going out," Eugene said. "Wanna come with?"

"Where?" I asked.

"Bed," he said.

"Bed?"

Eugene laughed. "It's a club," he said. "In the Meatpacking District." He made intense, sustained eye contact. He was so beautiful it was hard to look at him. "Ah, you're too young, aren't you?"

"I have an ID," I said defensively.

"An ID!" he said. "You can come with us if you like."

I shook my head. "I should sleep for tomorrow," I said. "Meet-and-greet at the agency."

He nodded. "You'll come this weekend. You must experience New York!"

Past midnight, the apartment was empty. I lay on the floor, in a nest I'd made out of clothes staring up at a hairline crack that ran across the ceiling. Outside, I could hear horns honking and people shouting. Somehow I'd ended up in yet another boiling-hot room with no air-conditioning, but I was happy. I had come so far. Starting tomorrow, I was really going to be a model. And yet, I felt something else—fear. What if it didn't work out? What if I didn't make it?

I rummaged around in my backpack for my flip phone and dialed the number of the farmhouse in Andale. She picked up on the third ring. "Hello?"

"Hi, Mama," I said. "It's me."

"I know who it is, Lou Lou," she said. She sounded slurry; I knew she was drunk. Tears welled in my eyes. "You in a penthouse?" she said. "You got a butler yet?"

"No, Mom," I said. "I'm on a mattress on the floor. Your favorite."

"Sounds about right," she said.

"I'll let you know what happens this week," I said. I had to call her tomorrow; she was too far gone. "I just called to say I love you."

"Love you too," she said. "When are you coming to visit me?" There was sadness in her voice, something whimpering.

"Soon," I said. "I'll call you after my meeting with the agency tomorrow. I gotta go." I knew she would have tried to keep me on the phone longer, but I couldn't stand to hear her cry.

———————

I was still angry at her for calling me in as a runaway, even if it had turned out to be the most efficient way to get me out of a situation that had become untenable. I'd spent a month at the children's home in Wichita, which had the charm of a dentist's office and the warmth of an emergency room: cots in corners of rooms that resembled cells, overhead lighting like a convenience store bathroom, plastic plants. The courtyard window was covered in bars. A kid with half his head shaved had his hands taped up so he wouldn't chew his fingernails off. Every week, Clinton or Mo would bring me clean clothes and wave at me through a set of locked glass doors. I was the only boy there who wasn't in any criminal trouble—I was just another small-town runaway, which I imagined was the title written next to my name on the registration form. In class, a counselor passed out worksheets for the day, and we did endless multiplication assignments, which looked like they were at an elementary-school level. Math was my worst subject, but this wasn't hard. And yet, when I looked around, I could see the other boys were struggling. Whatever neglect they'd suffered had been worse than mine. My childhood hadn't been easy, but I'd always had school, if nothing else. I had taken so much for granted. I would have rather been back at the farmhouse, with its drafty walls and ice-cold showers, in the chaos of what my mom had created, but how could I go home again after everything that had happened between us?

After nearly four weeks, one of the counselors told me that my mom was coming to pick me up.

"What?" I said. "Why? I can't go back there."

"You're not," she said. "We've had many conversations with her and come to the conclusion that you'll be better off living with your sister."

"Meadow? She's in Florida."

"Looks like you're getting exactly what you've been telling everyone you want," she said. "You're getting out of Kansas."

I waited for her in the lobby of the children's home until I saw Joe's Buick LeSabre pull up in the parking lot, flattening a patch of dandelion weeds. My mom was in the front seat, wearing her grapefruit-sized diva sunglasses and a long floral dress, with a drawstring tie across her chest, and a bonnet with an enormous plastic bow. She looked like she was going to the Kentucky Derby. Was all of this a joke to her? As I climbed into the back seat, carrying my clothes in grocery bags, I wanted her to hug me, to say that she had missed me, but she said nothing, and so neither did I. All we could hear was the clicking of the turn signal. I'd played out the conversation in my head, the things I would say. "How could you desert me like that?" I'd howl. "You drunk bitch. I was going to school. I was doing what I was supposed to do. And you get me locked up in this hellhole?" I wanted to call her every name in the book. I wanted to tell her that her hair looked terrible from the box dye she'd done the night before, even though it didn't. But I knew how that conversation would end. She always fought fire with fire. She would have won.

After only a month, Andale looked different to me somehow—the vastness of the cornfields, rows of golden flames. It seemed bigger but also smaller. The sound of a harmonica drifted from the radio as my mom smoked, a wisp of it vanishing out the crack of the window. Although we were driving back in, I felt sure that I was being driven out.

Back at the farmhouse, my mom sat at the kitchen table. She'd taken off the tablecloth, probably because it had too many holes burned in it, and it made the old wooden table feel strangely new. She didn't cry, and neither did I, even though we both knew I was leaving and I might not come back. Meadow hadn't been able to take time off from work to come and get me—she was a captain in the Air Force, having enlisted when she was seventeen—so she had called our older sister, Summer, who lived back in Arkansas, who in turn had roped her husband, David, into driving to Andale to pick me up and drop me off in Florida. As I loaded my things into his car, I wondered if it would always be like this.

And I wondered how my mom had pitched this to Meadow, since her relationship with Meadow was even more toxic than with me. I could practically hear the slurry phone call, whatever lie she'd made up. "Colton's up and run away," she would have said. "No one knows where he is. Somebody's gonna take my baby. Please, Meadow. Don't abandon him. We have to do whatever we can to protect Colton. He's young and he's gay and after I find him, he needs to get out of here." My Social Security checks were an added bonus, as they would go to my guardian, so that must have helped in the negotiation process.

I said goodbye to Clinton last. He was the only person in my family who could face my mom without getting into a knock-down, drag-out fight. He was happy as long as she was around. I hugged him so tightly, it felt like one of our heads was going to pop off.

"Remember who did this?" I said to him. "Mom. She's the reason that we're being ripped apart." He started to cry, and I did too, and we stood there for a minute, hugging each other, both of us crying uncontrollably—until I heard David start the engine and knew it was time to go.

I was nervous about living with Meadow. She was twenty-one now, and she lived on the Florida Panhandle, in a town called Navarre, about thirty minutes from Pensacola and right outside Eglin Air Force Base. She'd bought an inexpensive house in a quiet neighborhood near the ocean, which impressed me. She'd grown up fast, and her skin was thicker than anyone's I'd ever met. She loved to drop military jargon in casual conversation—BDU, IFC, UWA—even though she knew that no civilian knew what she was talking about, but she couldn't care less. When I looked at her in confusion, she'd roll her eyes and give me a look like, "Ugh, you're so stupid." I hadn't seen her much over the last few years since she'd enlisted, and in the passenger seat of David's Jeep, after a long car ride, I felt pangs of anxiety.

But Meadow's house turned out to be the calmest environment I'd ever called home. I had my own bedroom, with an air conditioner to cut the Florida humidity, and there was a dresser that she had bought just for me, a place for me to put my clothes, a place for me to fold my underwear and not have to worry about Clinton stealing it, a dresser that would house my belongings for the first time in my life. As I unpacked my things—the Hollister and Abercrombie polos that Meadow would send me on every holiday, all striped and clean and new-looking—I thought for the first time that everything was going to be okay. I would be a better person here. She'd bought me an alarm clock too, which I ended up not using, because she'd wake me up early to drop me off at school on her way to the base so I wouldn't have to ride the bus. There was a framed photo on the nightstand of the two of us taken a few years earlier. She'd been blond then, but she was constantly dyeing her hair—red, auburn, gold, light brown, caramel streaks. We'd all inherited my mother's vanity.

Meadow was strict. She was always grounding me for something—over a scratch on her Lexus, which I wasn't allowed to drive in the first place, or for not knowing that Paris was in France, which got me two more weeks, or for taking a picture with my head in a copy machine at school, or for wasting ink from her inkjet printer. She invoiced me forty-five dollars for a new ink cartridge after I did that, even though my Social Security checks were already going directly to her. There was no community theater program, only the productions that were put on at school, which lacked the prestige I was craving. I sleepwalked through my classes. And it was as if as soon as I was away from my mom, I needed her again; I started calling her every day. We couldn't forgive each other for what we had done to one another, but we also couldn't disentangle ourselves. Even though we never talked explicitly about what happened that terrible night at the farmhouse, I knew she had accepted that I was gay.

The same question I'd asked in Kansas had followed me all the way to Florida: *How the hell am I going to get out of here?* Without acting as an option, I'd reset my sights on the modeling industry. My body was changing: I had begun to look like a man in photographs, although not in person yet, and I'd hit a growth spurt that felt to me like fifty feet in height, although really I was topping out at five eight. I started digging around online for all the information I could find about how to get an agent—a real one this time. If I could start modeling, I thought, I'd get to travel the world, work with photographers I'd studied for years on Models.com, work with people who loved fashion as much as I did—never mind that to me, "fashion" meant a Hollister polo and a bucket hat. As a model, I'd get to learn on the job while getting paid. Besides, I'd watched so many episodes of *America's Next Top Model* that I was sure I had all the primary skills down.

On weekends, I roped a friend who had a decent film camera into taking pictures of me. We would crawl along the beaches of the Florida Panhandle like seductive mermen washing up to shore, wearing brightly colored tank tops, trucker hats, and stonewashed denim, because what's sexier than wet jeans? Then we would immediately take the film to the local Walgreens to get it developed, practically ripping the envelope out of the cashier's hands and then scurrying to a back aisle to sit on the floor and assess our work. I was the girl with all the potential in the world, and Tyra had just one photo left in her hands.

My favorite modeling website compiled lists of the top models in all categories—commercial, supers, sexiest, fresh faces—along with industry news and agency directories. One night, I finally got up the courage to look up the agency addresses and their submission requirements.

- All aspiring male models must fit the height requirements of 5'11"–6'2".
- Please include four digital photos, taken with no makeup, no hair products. One from the front, two profile shots to show facial structure, one full body in white briefs or boxer briefs.

- Can include 3 "professional" photos if available.
- Please include an email address where we can contact you if interested.

I was five foot eight on a good day, but I wasn't going to let something as trivial as that get in the way of my career in fashion. After all, it hadn't stopped Kate Moss. And I probably wasn't done growing yet. Ignoring that detail, which I had decided was not particularly consequential, I took digital photos of myself with my sister's camera while she was at work, propping it on the kitchen counter and setting the self-timer to ten seconds. I stood on my tiptoes just out of frame to make myself look taller and angled my body as much as I could, arching my back and pulling my long hair out of my face like a Victoria's Secret model. It would not have crossed my mind that it might be unwise to send photos of myself, at age fifteen, wearing tiny white briefs with a visible dick print, to strangers. I'd already done so much worse.

I didn't tell Meadow what I was doing—after all, if somebody actually signed me, surely I'd be going away for the summer. And even if I were to get signed, I knew from my research that it would be a two-year contract for representation that wouldn't guarantee me work, only that I would get castings for possible work. So I did what came naturally to me: I lied. On the applications, I said that I was five foot eleven.

Within a week, I had an email back from one of the agencies I'd applied to—not just one of them, but the best modeling agency in the world: DNA. They represented Naomi Campbell, Linda Evangelista, and Adriana Lima. They arranged a phone call and asked me to send a video of me posing and runway walking, which I did, and then they offered me a contract. It was that simple—

weirdly simple, easier than it felt like it should have been. Even more serendipitously, Meadow had an eight-week training program already booked for the summer, and she'd been worried about what I was going to do while she was away. A perfect solution: I'd spend the summer working in New York, where, we were assured, I'd be very well supervised. After I'd sent in some additional photos and information, they sent me a plane ticket. It was my first time being on a plane.

When I awoke in the morning my first day in New York, I felt knots in my back, then knots in my stomach. It was the worst night's sleep I'd gotten since I lived at the farmhouse. I rolled over only to discover that Eugene was lying in bed next to me, snoring gently. Oh God—had I hooked up with him already? No—that hadn't happened; he was unfortunately straight. He had just passed out on the other side of my mattress, probably too drunk to get up to the top bunk.

I watched him sleep for a moment. He was wearing designer briefs. He had James Dean hair, bushy eyebrows, a sun-kissed jaw, and lips that looked stung with venom. I wanted to run my thumb down them in slow motion. A thin trail of prickly hair ran down his chest and beneath his waistband. Maybe I would be desired by others the way I desired him.

Walking toward SoHo, where my agency was headquartered, the streets were still wet with rain but the sun was shining. I was wearing my favorite ripped, paint-splattered Hollister jeans, a white American Eagle T-shirt with a silver bird emblem, a belt with an oversized buckle, and boots that I'd padded with socks, held tightly together with gray duct tape, to give me an extra three inches or so of height. I would do whatever I could to keep the lie going that I was tall enough. But I was nervous. In the lobby, I gave my name

to the receptionist and waited for a minute. The space felt cold
and bitchy and chic. Iconic stories had been told there. I imagined
a young Naomi Campbell sitting in that same foyer. Finally, I was
escorted back through a set of frosted green, tempered-glass doors.
It looked like I was heading into a forest.

By this point I was hobbling; I couldn't quite walk in my makeshift heels yet—emphasis on *yet*—and I couldn't remember the last
time I'd eaten. Standing, watching me stagger in, was my agent,
John. We'd spoken on the phone by that point, but we hadn't met
in person. He was short, scrappy, and balding; I had the sense that
he had pulled out his hair from nerves. He was also, I'd come to
discover, straight, which meant that my usual tricks wouldn't work
on him. As I approached him, I saw anger flicker across his face.
Oh shit.

"John, this is—" the receptionist began.

"Colton," John said. "Follow me." He turned on his heels and
walked briskly toward a glass conference room, and I followed
him in.

"Why are you walking like that?" he said.

"Walking like what?"

"Like you're in a pair of stilettos."

I felt my face flush. I thought about all the girls on *Top Model*—
how would they handle this? "It's my signature walk," I said.

His face darkened. "Take off your shoes," he said.

I froze. I was about to be found out. But the only way out
was through. Begrudgingly, I unlaced my boots and stepped out
of them, feeling the heavy weight of the duct-taped rolls of socks
beneath my heels. I stood, flat-footed, on the ground.

"You're short," he said.

"No," I said. "I'm the right height."

"You're not," he said, scowling. "What a colossal waste of time. If you don't book anything this trip, you're not coming back." He opened the door to the conference room. "Eddie, Tyler!" he called. Two gays scuttled in. "Take Colton's measurements," John said. "And get his *actual* height."

One of the gays pulled out a tape and wrapped it around my waist. "Congrats on dropping the baby fat," he trilled. "Hard work paying off!" The other gay nodded in agreement. I wondered how many other young men and women just like me had come from the Midwest chasing a dream that would fade quicker than a spray tan. But I was convinced that I was different—that I had what it took, and if I could just get in front of the right people, they would want to book me. I would prove John wrong.

After being instructed to go into the bathroom for fifteen minutes to practice my faces, they led me by the arm up the black iron steps that spiraled from the sixth floor up to the roof to take some Polaroids to send to clients. The rooftop was vast, and the day was gorgeous, the light filtering through skyscrapers so close that I could have fixed my hair in the reflection of their glossy exteriors. I stood against a concrete wall and they fired off directions: *Stop pouting your lips! Look angry! Look happy! Look sad!* In those pictures I look almost waifish, and my eyes are as pure and blue as the ocean, but there's also something sexual about them—a come-hither stare. In most of them, I had my shirt off, and you can see my ribs poking through my chest. I'd have looked like a carcass that had been starved to death were it not for the fire I was kindling in my eyes. And most importantly, in the pictures—whether it was the angle or the lighting or the way I was holding my body—I looked tall.

Now I had castings, which were called "go-sees." I carried a book that said DNA on the cover—a portfolio of all my photos. You could easily spot a model on the street—they were carrying a satchel, or just holding their book, although you had to be careful, because the sun would melt the plastic on the pages, which would stick to the photographs and ruin them, and you were charged a fee to replace them. Mine only had the Polaroids that had been taken on the roof of DNA, which I was told would be exciting to some clients, that I was the new girl in town—fresh meat in a city full of carnivores.

I took the subway uptown to my first casting, which was for Abercrombie & Fitch—technically for their kids' line, since I was too young to shoot adult Abercrombie, but the castings were held at the same time, and the photos were more youthful and less sala-cious than the notoriously sexual photos that had made the brand infamous. There was a long line of models, at least twenty of them, and they all looked like men, with square jaws and military haircuts, wearing white wife-beaters. An enormous corkboard was covered in comp cards—like business cards for models, with a picture and their measurements—organized by brand: Hollister, Gilly Hicks, Abercrombie & Fitch, Abercrombie Kids. It was like a map of the stars. Inside the studio, the space was bright white and sterile, with makeshift walls to bounce the natural light from the window onto the other walls. This was dazzling to me. The space had actually been designed to make everyone look as good as possible. It was a room where you couldn't take a bad photo.

As I approached the front of the line where three casting direc-tors were reviewing models' books, I saw that some models were just being dismissed with a polite "Thanks for coming in." But the model ahead of me, they took a little more time to review—then I heard one of the casting directors asking him if he could go into the

bathroom and put some water in his hair so they could take a picture of him looking wet. He obliged and came out dripping, his hair
slicked back as if he'd just emerged from a lake. My hands were
shaking as my turn was called.

"Next!" I approached the table and stood there silently, resist-
ing the impulse to make small talk as the woman at the table appraised me. At the agency, I'd been given strict instructions not to
take up more time than was necessary.

"Where are you from?" she asked.

"Kansas," I said.

"You're not in Kansas anymore," she said.

I laughed as if I had never heard that before.

She pulled down her glasses and studied me. I held my breath.
Then—

"Would you mind stepping into the restroom and putting some
water in your hair?"

I grinned. "I wouldn't mind at all," I said.

In the bathroom, I looked at my reflection in the mirror: my
high cheekbones, my wide eyes, my pouting lips. I would not be
going back to Kansas, getting a job at Sonic, telling stories forever
about my failed attempts to make it in the big city while I sat on
a tailgate, drinking a Miller High Life. A droplet of water dripped
down my forehead, then landed on the edge of the sink. I smiled
my biggest, brightest smile and tried to feel beautiful.

Living in the city was invigorating—going from one casting to the
next, free dinners I never finished paid for by the promoters, partying at clubs with Eugene. The clubs in New York weren't like Big
Daddy's. They were stylish, full of models and celebrities. Going

with Eugene and his promoter friend Denise, we would get pulled out of line and ushered to the back of the club and the best tables. Seated on the banquette, looking out at the sea of beautiful faces, I felt like I had made it. I didn't realize that the partying was its own full-time job—that we were being used as pretty faces by the promoters to add sex appeal to their venues, which would in turn bring in better clientele who would spend real money, the kind of money I didn't have.

But it was also wearying, for so many reasons. I was running on fumes; I don't think I had a square meal all summer. I was convinced that if I couldn't be a muscular male model, I had to be more androgynous and childlike, and being thin was the best way to accomplish that, and so I ate very little, as little as I possibly could. I wanted my cheekbones to pop, my clavicle to jut, to be as fashionably angular as I could. Kate Moss had popularized heroin chic; I was sure I could get there without any drugs.

The other problem was that now I had debt—a lot of it. Signing with an agency, you accrue debt in the form of the rent for your model apartment, which is typically a space that the agency owns, but they hike up the rent for its tenants, and then take that out of what you're paid when you book a job—payment that takes upward of six months to receive. Printing photos for your book gets put into your debt; the hosting of your portfolio on the agency's website gets put into your debt. Then a 20 percent commission in most markets, but 70 percent in Paris—yikes. I never knew what I was being charged for; I didn't even have access to the account. I was just periodically sent an email saying how much I still owed the agency.

Early in the mornings, still wired from being out partying and only sleeping a few hours, I would go into a magazine shop by the

agency offices and flip through the titles. It was incredible to me
that here there were entire stores dedicated to high-fashion magazines, a little hole-in-the-wall on Houston between a dive bar and a
coffee shop that carried all these titles the rest of the world barely
knew existed: *Numéro, Rollacoaster, L'officiel Hommes*. There were
so many pieces of art in the pages of those issues. I knew that the
other guys in the model house didn't love it the way I did, didn't
revere the craft of modeling, didn't take it seriously. I remember
flipping through *V Magazine* and seeing Eugene and a few of my
other roommates in an iconic spread: fifty of the top models in the
industry standing together to form a giant letter *V* in the middle of
Sheep's Meadow. I rushed back to show them, after paying almost
fifty dollars to get them each their own copy. Eugene looked at me
and said, "Another free editorial, on another long day." Editorials
didn't pay—they were more to build a rapport with photographers
and the magazine. It was just a job for them, a way to make money
until they found their true callings. But it was art to me. I wanted
to feel the way I looked in my photographs, confident and alluring.
I wanted to learn from the best. But I hadn't booked a job all
summer.

Leaving a casting one afternoon, I began sobbing, right there
on Mercer Street. It started with a wave of hunger, then turned
into a rush of panic, so great that I felt like I was going to faint in
the middle of oncoming traffic. I sat down on the sidewalk, feeling
like the only person in the city. Everyone had places to go, things to
do; the rat race of daily living in New York was so normal to them. I
couldn't do it anymore.

I dug around in my backpack for my cell phone and called
my mom. She sounded sober. That was weird. "I can't do this," I
sobbed. "Nobody loves me here."

"Do you want me to come out there?" she said.

"No," I cried. "I don't have any money. Neither do you."

"I can figure it out, baby."

I shook my head back and forth, rocking on the ground. "I don't know what to do," I said. "I just don't know what to do."

A few days later, I got a call from my agents that I'd booked Abercrombie. I called my mom again. "Does it pay?" she asked. She sounded worried.

"Yeah," I said. "Five to seven thousand dollars, depending on how long they keep me." Never mind that it would all go toward paying off my nebulous debt.

"I thought you were losing it," she said. "I thought you couldn't do this anymore."

"I was. I mean, I can. I'm trying."

"Are you lying to me about this?" she asked.

"No, Mom."

"You eating? Getting into trouble?"

"Yes. No."

"Call me when you get there."

The shoot was with Bruce Weber for the Abercrombie Kids holiday campaign, and it was to take place in Bangor, Maine. At the gate at the airport, I spotted two other models who had to be headed for the same place: They were brawny but angular, like young Greek gods. Descending through the foggy clouds of Maine on a little flight from New York, the misty view looked spooky, as if vampires might live there.

It turned out most of the models for the shoot had been on the flight, as I discovered when we scoped each other out at baggage claim; there were fifteen of us, all of us striking, the boys athletic and fresh-faced, the girls slender and wholesome, milling around the lobby like a pack of fawns. The energy wasn't competitive; instead everyone was friendly, far from home and hungry to make a connection. "I have a fake ID if you guys want me to get us some beers later," I volunteered, trying to establish some social currency, and all those beautiful faces nodded back at me.

The liquor store was in the middle of town, which looked like something out of a storybook—lush green forests, pale people driving their Mercedes down cobblestone streets, glowing lampposts. I'd never been anywhere like this before, a place that was draped in a misty haze. Using my per diem, I bought cheap vodka, Natty Light, a carton of cigarettes, and red Solo cups with ping-pong balls so we could play beer pong. They didn't even ask to see my ID. It was as if it were normal in a small town like this for underage models to buy alcohol.

Back at the hotel, I hosted the party in my room. The floors had plaid carpet in orange and auburn like fall leaves; I imagined them crunching underfoot. We moved the beds to form a makeshift table for beer pong and began playing music. Not long after, there was a knock on the door; one of the other models had called housekeeping to bring up ice for the warm beer, and the woman behind the door didn't look happy at the sight of fifteen underage models, lean as gazelles, crowded into a room full of alcohol.

Forty minutes later, there was another knock on the door— louder this time, more like a banging. "Police! Open up!" someone barked.

"Shit!" one of the models said.

I opened the door and two police officers were standing there. "Whose room is this?" one of them asked.

"Mine," I said, thinking I could talk my way out of it. I looked back over my shoulder at the other models. There were red Solo cups lined in triangles on either side of the desk.

"Put your hands behind your back," one of them said, and I felt handcuffs click around my wrists. I'd felt that sensation before, with Damon, but this was different. They pulled me out of the room and led me down the hallway. *Fuck,* I thought. I was gonna be in so much trouble with my agents, and I wasn't going to be able to do the shoot tomorrow. All this, just for trying to have a little fun and to make some friends and let loose a little bit. Why was I always like this? Why was I always such an agent of chaos?

The police led me through the lobby in handcuffs and out toward a cop car idling in the parking lot. As they pushed me into the back seat, I saw one of the handlers from Abercrombie running out the front door of the hotel, looking harried. His name was Carlos; I'd met him at the first casting in New York. I saw him gesticulating as he pleaded with the police. *Sir, please. No, I promise. Isn't there anything we can do?* I couldn't make out everything he was saying from inside the cop car, but I found out later that he was pushing the local business angle: All you really had to do was explain you were with a production supporting the local economy, and people would usually go easy on you.

A few minutes later, I was being uncuffed and written a ticket—for being a minor in possession. It came with a hefty fine and would stay on my record for the next four years. But I managed to avoid getting taken down to the station. As he escorted me up to my room, Carlos was talking at a rapid clip. "We knew you were going to be trouble," he said, shaking his head. "Do not tell your agents this happened. Do not tell anyone on set tomorrow that this happened. If you do, you will be in a lot of trouble, and

I can promise you that you will never be asked back on an Abercrombie shoot again, do you understand me?" Something about the way he was talking to me tipped me off that this had likely happened before; I wasn't the first teen terror to wreak havoc on set. But I had established my status with the other models. I was officially a legend.

The next day, we were taken to the location for the actual shoot, which was impossibly picturesque: rolling green hills, fields with rustic log cabins blanketed in fog, tall grass, and grazing horses that had been hired to be on set with us—equine models. Their handlers were dressed like an Abercrombie catalog too—in a collegial, equestrian style. Everyone working there—the stylists, the glam team, even the caterers—looked rich. Hamptons rich. Long hair braided into one long fishtail, minimal makeup but glowing. Some of the models looked gawky and odd, storklike; they were the ones who would go on to have high-fashion careers, even if they didn't have the standard Americana feel that you saw in the Abercrombie catalog. And then there were models who didn't look beautiful when you stared directly at them, but came to life in a photograph.

At base camp, there was a makeshift tent that resembled a teepee, full of clothes and props—canoes and oars and lacrosse sticks and croquet mallets and colorful balls and nets and footballs and Aztec blankets. We tried on outfits, pairing them with different props. The setup was so elaborate, it looked like a pop-up town in the middle of this picturesque wooded dreamland. There would be two days of shoots before they made cuts. If you got cut, you'd be paid $5,000; if you lasted the whole week, you'd make $9,000. We waited in the tent for Bruce's assistant to come grab us, one by one, to shoot us.

I was wearing a blue plaid button-up with low-rise dark-wash jeans with holes in the knees and brown flip-flops and glasses—approved by Abercrombie corporate—when Bruce's assistant tapped me on the shoulder. "Colton, you're being invited to set," he said. A wave of relief flooded over me: I was worried they'd found out about the previous night and they were going to punish me by not shooting me at all.

Bruce shook my hand. He had a white beard and a bandanna tied around his head.

"Turn your head to the right, Colton," he said. I did as he asked, startled that he knew my name.

"Now take the glasses off," he said. I did. "Mess your hair up," he said. "And now back up against that tree." Right then, as he slowly raised his camera to meet my gaze, it was as if something clicked besides the button of the camera. There was a mysterious connection between the eye of the camera and me, something electric. It felt like we were moving in unison, like we were dancing together—Bruce, his camera, and me.

Reflexively, I came down to my knees as he continued shooting. I began crawling in the tall grass on my hands and knees and tried to seduce the camera with my eyes. I heard him muttering to his assistant. "What do you want me to do next?" I asked, feeling the momentum starting to wane.

He sat there and studied me for a moment. I took off my flannel, so I was only wearing the T-shirt. "We can do some without my shirt?" I said.

"Of course," he said, as I began peeling it off. I continued crawling through the brush. I had never felt more powerful, more alive, more in control. Bruce shot me all day—with other boys, with girls, playing football. Was I finally someone's muse? He sat there clicking away with his camera, watching us dance the choreography of our youth. It was a performance, all affect, but it didn't matter. On film, it looked like the real thing.

Back in New York, John told me that I'd gotten a direct request, which was unusual; it wasn't a casting, but rather, a photographer had specifically requested me. His name was David Armstrong, and he was looking for new models to shoot for his upcoming coffee-table book.

"David doesn't like working with agencies," John said. "He doesn't shoot for big paychecks, or for magazines like *Vogue* anymore. He thinks that's all staged bullshit." There was a slightly sour look on his face, like he had hoped that I would fail so he could drop me for having lied to him about my height. "He doesn't like too many cooks in the kitchen. No styling. Nobody limits his art. He might ask you to do some risqué things."

I looked up the photographer online, and his work looked provocative—controversial. The boys in his pictures appeared prepubescent, but the way they were photographed was erotic. They wore little clothing, sometimes no clothing at all. That style of photography didn't appeal to me. I liked crisp, overly edited Steven Meisel photography where you didn't know whether you were looking at a human being or a lifelike piece of artificial intelligence. But whatever risqué things John was talking about couldn't be any worse than the things I'd done in Kansas.

The morning of the shoot, I looked at the instructions I'd written down on a piece of paper, the subways I had to take; I couldn't afford to travel by cab. Living in New York felt like a perpetual math problem. I was always late, always sweating, always disheveled and harried. My only saving grace was that in the modeling world, if your appointment was at 2:00 p.m., you wouldn't be seen until 4:00 p.m., so it never really mattered. I navigated my way to Williamsburg on the subway and got off at the Lorimer stop, then followed the directions and walked far longer than I'd expected—it felt like miles. I turned a corner and found I was on a street of abandoned warehouses, cavernous and industrial. The sun illuminated the dust particles kicked up by the wind. The day looked full of magic. Had I been tricked, taken a wrong turn? It didn't seem like anyone lived here.

Finally I arrived at an old Gothic house, three stories high. I had never seen a house like that in New York; it looked like a place my mom might dream of living—another dusty trail, languishing and historic, like at one point it had been beautiful, hosted lavish dinner parties, people chuckling over martinis clotted with olives, and when all the people had gone away, the old matriarch would still be inside, quilting and watching her programs. The windows were cracked, but it still had a glow about it.

I knocked on the front door and was greeted by a slender man with wide, gargoyle-like features. His long black hair and pale skin gave him the appearance of a penguin. He brought me back to a small vacant bedroom, which had a mattress with no sheets.

"You can put your stuff here," he said softly. "This will be your room for the day."

The other rooms in the house each seemed to have a different theme, as though the building was more a set than a place anyone actually lived. In a sitting room, I perched on an orange crushed-velvet couch, and he brought me a glass of water. I waited in silence.

Finally, an older man, maybe sixty, came in. He was feeble-looking, in a cardigan, with mussed-up salt-and-pepper hair and glasses. He looked a bit like Mr. Monopoly, a caricature, an odd bird. "Hello," he said. His voice was kind, but he was already focused.

I looked at him looking at me. His eyes scanned me. It felt like he was doing surgery on my appearance, not in a critical way, but like he was preparing for something. He looked to me and to the window, then up to the lights, and then back across the old banister that spiraled around the staircase. For a moment I was a pawn in the chess game of his house, another strange thing taking up space here in his visual world. He looked at my face, considered the light, anticipated different angles. But I didn't feel judged. I felt seen.

He brought out two costumes: a pair of red briefs with a tiny, firm waistline that he'd paired with a military jacket with epaulets; and a leather harness with a choker plus an S&M-style ball gag. "Are you comfortable wearing this?" he asked. I nodded. I had been warned that it might be provocative. Yet there was something different about the energy of him—something loving. He didn't want anything tactile or immediate from me, from my body, from my face. He only wanted to capture it in his photographs. I knew that instinctively. I trusted him.

"Can you lie down on the bed?" he said. There were no big studio lights, no equipment. Just me and him and his camera. "Look up at the ceiling," he said. "Be calm. Be natural." And as he began to shoot I felt like a little boy again, and whether I was making it up or really connecting with something inside him, I suddenly felt certain that he had been treated the way I had growing up, that the same sort of things that had happened to me had also happened to him. That this was why he took pictures the way he did—not to be sexy, but to comment on sex, on the way that we are sexualized, on the gaze held by the camera, on beauty not as an amplifier of desire but as a question. Why do we lust? When does a child become an adult? When are we allowed to desire them?

"Stop posing," he said. "You don't have to try to be beautiful. Be natural." Natural beauty—what a strange and impossible thing that was. I couldn't see myself as beautiful, no matter how other people saw me. I wanted Photoshop, ring lights, flashbulbs, drama—all those things that maximized the beauty that others saw in me, pushing out my neck, sucking in my cheeks, making myself skinny, trying to be more like what I thought beauty was supposed to be, what a model was supposed to be. But every time I tried to model, he asked me to stop the show.

I couldn't put it into words then, but it was the first time I could remember that a man had looked at my face, looked at my body, and not wanted to take something from me.

SCHERTZ, TEXAS
2005

A dive motel. This one in Schertz, Texas, a drive-by town full of drive-thrus, just off the main highway that connected San Antonio and Austin. I carried my last box from the room to Meadow's car, a 2002 Chevy Blazer, and placed it carefully in the back seat, looking at the things I had collected: cups I had gotten on a class trip, a plastic watch, napkins and key chains from places I had visited, loose change, bubble gum, burnt CDs, Polaroids from my summer in New York, the comp cards of Kate Moss I had stolen from my modeling agency, and then a few of my own, the ones I had brought back so I could show the kids at my new school in Texas how I spent my summers. One more year. Just one more year of school and I'd be out.

It was my senior year of high school, and we were moving—again. Meadow had been stationed in Texas, so if I wanted to have a solid roof over my head and finish high school, spending this last year with her after my summer in New York was the only option. She'd bought a house—it was easy to get a military loan, and she didn't like wasting money—but it was in a new development that hadn't been completed yet, so we'd been crashing in this motel while they finished construction.

Meadow looked irritable as she dragged the last of her things down the steps from our room. I felt like a burden, probably because I had become one. My dreams were waiting for me in New York, but I would have to graduate high school to realize them.

"Be careful with the door," Meadow said as we got into the car. "Don't hit the door on the other car like you always do."

"I did that one time three years ago, Meadow," I snapped. "God, you're just like Mom."

"Why are you so pissy when I'm the only one taking care of you?" she said.

"Taking care of me? I've been paying your bills since I moved in!"

"Your father's Social Security doesn't go that far, Colton." She gripped the steering wheel. I should have been grateful: She could have let me become a foster kid or end up homeless. We both knew our mom wasn't stable enough to be my guardian. But still I resented her, probably because she was an adult, and I wanted desperately to be treated like one too.

Schertz was full of unused golf courses built to attract buyers to the homes tucked behind the second hole, highway motels for tired truckers and sex workers, and my least favorite feature of

Texas—megachurches. Meadow's house was in a golf community, which she had chosen because they were building a mall nearby soon, which would add resale value when it came time for her to sell; she was always so strategic about things like that, such an adult.

Driving through the big gates, past the golf course, we were suddenly surrounded by rows and rows of manufactured homes, brick and plasticky white wood, many of them still being built. But her house had new, fluffy beige carpet, and it still smelled like fresh paint, promising and unsullied. I was sick of starting over, but I mustered enough enthusiasm to smile. She'd had to navigate another complicated legal situation to tell the school that she was my guardian and she'd dealt with Social Services on my behalf, none of which I envied.

"The house is great, Meadow," I said. "Thank you." I imagined making new friends, maybe inviting them over, not being embarrassed of where I lived, even though Meadow probably wouldn't allow that. I was used to going over to other people's houses, seeing how they lived their lives, meeting their families, befriending their siblings, looking into their closets to see the clothes they wore, hearing about their memories. It was so much more comfortable to be a visitor in other people's lives than to let them into mine. What if they saw the chaos—what if they found out about my troubled past and got close enough to see the cracks in my façade? Would they accept me? Or would they see that I felt like nothing more than a stranger in my own home—a home that wasn't really even mine?

The high school was gigantic—nearly ten times as many students as had been in Andale. I had thought the kids in Texas would be hillbillies, but thankfully, I was wrong. I joined the tennis team and the theater club, which would give me things to do—places where I belonged. But even in a school that size, I was something of a curiosity—a working model who also played sports and was openly gay? I had stopped trying to stay closeted in Florida, and for the most part, nobody there had bothered me much. But in Schertz, one of the football players soon set his sights on me.

His name was Tyler, and he looked like a dog—a boxer, more specifically, like he had done too many blacked-out face plants at house parties and it had smushed his features together. He was six foot four, with spiky blond hair, and was built like a brick house. "Faggot," he'd say as I passed him in the hallway. I had to nip this in the bud if I was going to survive; I needed to become popular enough to squeak by.

I began keeping a log of what he was wearing and bullying Meadow into buying me the same clothes: preppy jock apparel from Abercrombie & Fitch and Hollister, the same kind of things I already wore. He favored a pink polo shirt from Abercrombie with small white stripes; I bought the same one and kept it in my locker. On days he would wear that to school, I would change into it, to make sure everyone saw Tyler was wearing the same thing as the gay kid.

"Nice shirt, girl," I said, swishing past him in the hallway. "Looking fierce." His football buddies laughed. How could they not? It was funny.

During Spirit Week, at the powder puff game, where the boys wore crop tops and played volleyball and the girls played football in full regalia, I finally bested him by crushing a right side spike directly into his face. After the match, he lifted me up over his shoulder and carried me around the gymnasium, like I was as light as a football. I was sure he was going to slam me to the ground, but he didn't. It was his way of telling me that he would leave me alone.

I needed a way to make money in the interim so I could get the hell out of Texas. I applied to fast-food restaurants, but nobody would hire me because I had so few available hours: I was in school full-time, and I played sports. Finally, the burger chain Red Robin agreed to hire me as a busboy for nine dollars an hour. But not long after I started, I noticed that they had a mascot in a costume roaming the restaurant: He wore yellow tights and an outfit with a giant beak, orange-yellow and red. He was dancing with kids and having fun. I asked my manager if I could do that instead.

"What?" he said. "Why? Nobody ever wants to do that job."

"Why not?" I said. "Look at how much fun he's having! He's doing the funky chicken in a costume! That's hilarious!"

He gave me a look like I was weird. "Sure," he said. "You can be the mascot." That job paid thirteen dollars an hour.

———

In computer class, I noticed all the other kids were spending a lot of time on Myspace—updating their profile pictures, changing their backgrounds, adding music, chatting with one another. I began posting my modeling photos on my own. The friend requests began pouring in: not just friends from school, but also complete strangers. I always just accepted the requests.

At lunch one day, in the computer lab, I was reviewing the comments on my most recent photo when I noticed that I had a direct message from a guy named Jay whose location had him in a suburb a few miles away. "New in town?" it said. He was nineteen, and his photos weren't like those of the other guys who messaged me. His eyes were gentle, but his nose looked like he'd just taken a right hook to the face; I imagined that he'd be able to protect me when I couldn't protect myself. He was tall, ripped, and grinning like he didn't know there was a camera on him. He collected Pokémon figurines, had photos of himself making some of his own, and had no discernible style: like he was unassuming, unpretentious, unself-conscious.

"I am," I said. "Are you also in high school? You don't look like a high school kid." He didn't: He looked like a man.

"I graduated two years ago and I still live with my parents," he said. "But I'm about to move to Austin. We should go sometime. Are your pictures real?"

"Maybe you should drive here and you can see for yourself," I said.

I sat in the computer lab, my heart pounding. My sexuality was primal—it was never the feeling of butterflies in my heart, wishing a boy would pick me up after school and take me out for a soda. I wanted him inside me, to belong to him.

I went searching on Google to find out more about Jay. He had a sister who was two years older, but they could have been twins; they were both skyscraper-tall, athletic, and toned, like Olympic long jumpers. His parents looked kind. His dad was handsome, with white hair, a muscular build, and a big smile. His mom looked like she drove a minivan; maybe she was an English teacher at a school. They looked happy together. They gazed into the lens of the camera with bright golden smiles, like they'd never known hardship. I wanted to be a part of their family. I wanted their normal.

I gave Jay my phone number, and he offered to drive to Schertz and meet me that Friday after tennis practice. He would see me playing, note how athletic I was, and fall in love with me.

Toward the end of practice, I saw a car pull up across from the court—a black Chevrolet Monte Carlo. I was wearing shorter shorts that hit above the knee; I tried to move gracefully from my backhand to my forehand, squatting a little to emphasize my ass. When I finished practice, I walked over to the car just as he stepped out. He was tall, probably six foot three, and slender. He was wearing a T-shirt with characters in Japanese and enormous, baggy jeans, cinched with a belt made out of bottle caps. His hair was shaggy, and his nose was crooked. He looked like an anime character, or like he spent a lot of time in his basement playing video games. And he was clearly nervous. He looked like a work in progress. But I saw his potential.

I wanted to disarm him with my charm offensive. I gave him a hug. "Hey!" I said. "I'm Colton."

"You look better in person," he said shakily. His voice was high and a little nerdy.

"Thanks!" I said. "I appreciate that. Should we go?" I didn't want my tennis friends to see me getting into his car; I was worried about what they might think.

In the car, he talked to me about growing up Mormon—that he hadn't really dated either guys or girls before, which explained his nerves. Putting it together, I realized that he was probably a virgin. He had a loud, ridiculous laugh; it reminded me of bird-song. There was something childlike about him, unspoiled. I wasted no time putting my hand on the back of his head, trying to make him comfortable—which only seemed to make him more nervous. I saw sweat beading by his temples, which he kept wiping away distractedly. All the guys I had been with before were so confident in their sexuality; Jay was so nervous, but I found it endearing. Even though I was younger than him, I wanted to take care of him.

I'd planned to take him back to my house, since Meadow would be staying late on the base and I needed to shower, but when we pulled up, her car was in the driveway. *Shit*. Meadow opened the door still wearing her BDUs—her military getup—which made her, already a stern figure, even more threatening. "Who's this?" she said, eyes flashing.

"This is my friend Jay," I said. "Just stopping by really quick!" As I made my way upstairs, I heard her starting to give him the third degree: *So how old are you?* Poor guy. I showered quickly and rushed back downstairs in baggy jeans and a yellow tank top with splattered paint I'd made, because—fashion, duh. Meadow side-eyed me, a look that said, *You're really wearing that to the movies?* Just like my mom would have done.

"It was nice to meet you, Jay," she said. "You guys have fun. Be back by nine." I was pleasantly surprised that he'd managed to win her approval, nerves and all.

The movie was boring, something about superheroes, but our hands kept wandering closer to each other. Somewhere in the middle of the second half, I whispered to him, "Do you wanna leave?"

He looked at me in the dark. I could see the outlines of his handsome face. "Are you sure?" he asked.

"Yeah," I said. "It'll give us more time to get to know each other." I smiled what I thought was a slutty smirk, which he probably couldn't see in the low light.

"Sure," he said. "Let's go." He grabbed my hand and walked me out the side of the movie theater, which struck me as bold, particularly for Texas, where any public display of affection seemed audacious.

We made out in his car for a while, but when I put my hand on his bulge he froze up. "Is it okay if we take things a little slower?" he said. It wasn't my preference, but I nodded, and we went for a drive instead, cruising in circles around that little Texas town. He told me stories about his family, and I told him about my summer modeling in New York and my plans for the future. I wanted to move back to the city after high school to continue to model. "What do you want to do?" I asked him.

"Maybe figurines," he said. Off my confused expression, he continued: "I love making little things out of clay. Maybe something with comics. At the very least, I want to make some kind of art." It was sweet, and so deeply weird and foreign to my reality; I loved it. "People have said I could be a model too," he said. "But I don't really know if I have what it takes."

"Are you sure you're tall enough?" I said. He laughed and took my hand.

It was nearly nine now. I asked him to stop just before the house so Meadow wouldn't be watching us in the driveway as we pulled in. I climbed over the center console and mounted him. He was so much bigger than me, but also so innocent. Knowing that he was inexperienced only made me more confident: It felt like I could do no wrong, that everything would excite him. My hand slipped under the waistband of his boxers and just then—

"Can we wait?" he said.

"Yeah, if that's what you want."

"Maybe just not in a car. I don't know. I just want to take things slower on the first date. You know what I mean?"

"No big deal," I said. "I won't do anything you don't want me to do." I made my eyes as puppyish as possible, wanting him to throw the idea out the window, but he stood strong. And when it was time to go, he got out of the driver's side and opened the car door for me, like a true gentleman.

It felt strange to be doing something so chaste, especially with this treelike hunk of a man, after everything I had already been through sexually. Even though I was only seventeen, I felt like I'd had enough experience to know the way men saw me: that, with rare exceptions, my value was in the way I looked, and how I could be used for their sexual gratification. I liked it too, or so I thought, but even then I knew that I couldn't quite find the line between what I wanted because it felt good and what I wanted because it felt familiar. Did I want sex because I was a hormonal teenager, or did I want sex because it was the only way anyone had ever shown me I had value? I wasn't thinking about that yet, mostly because I was focused on getting Jay to fuck me, but it was lurking in our dynamic, something I would have to deal with eventually.

As we approached Meadow's house, I could see that she was standing with the front door open, watching. She had a funny expression on her face, like she was impressed that this guy was walking me to the door. But when we got there, he got nervous again. "Hi, Meadow!" he said in a high, anxious voice. Then he waved me goodbye, like he didn't want to hug me in front of her, turned, and walked back to his car.

I entered the house, shut the door behind me, and slid down to my butt on the floor, giggling. Meadow rolled her eyes. "Giddy as a schoolgirl," she said.

"I really like him," I said, and I watched her face soften.

Who needs the validation of social media when you have a real, live human boyfriend validating you all the time? For a little while, it was enough. I had never met anyone like Jay, who was so kind and so nurturing, such a true-blue nerd, who lavished me with attention as if I hung the moon. He wasn't trying to cultivate my insecurity or police my behavior; he just let me be me. It was the first time I'd ever had a boyfriend I really wanted to be around, as opposed to someone I needed for housing or security. I didn't even mind that all his clothes were adorned with anime characters. I wanted to suck his dick everywhere: in the dugout of the baseball field across the street from school; in his car; on one of the empty golf courses in town. I plastered my Myspace with photos of us. I thought he was so handsome and I wanted the world to see it.

One day I logged onto Myspace to find a message in my in-box from the account belonging to a magazine called *XY*. It was a popular underground gay magazine based in Los Angeles; I'd seen it at the newsstand I loved in New York, although it wasn't the kind of thing you could find in Texas. The note said:

> Hi Colton, We came across photos of you and your boyfriend Jay and wondered if it would be possible to shoot you both when we visit Austin, Texas. Let me know if that would interest you. We would just need parental signatures for you since we know you're not yet eighteen. Hope all is well—XY

My mind was blown. My Abercrombie shoot still hadn't come out; I had no confidence that it ever would. This was my opportunity to be in an actual magazine. It would be my ticket into the next chapter of my life. I burst out of my chair and ran outside to call Jay.

"Jay, go to your computer right now and look up *XY*," I said. "They just messaged me and they want to shoot us."

There was a long silence. "Colton, did you see these pictures?"

"Yeah!" I said. "I saw a couple of them. I mean, they're pretty underground, but if they had better subjects—like us—they could turn out something really cool and high fashion." I had heard the panelists talk this way on *America's Next Top Model*, and I was confident in my ability to parrot them convincingly.

"It looks so porny," he said.

"Oh," I said. This wasn't the reaction I had expected, and it bothered me. I knew that he was right, but why did it matter? We had the opportunity to be in a magazine. I wasn't going to be picky if this would help my career. "Well, I'll do it if you want to do it."

I heard him sigh. "I'll do anything for you, Colton. You know that. I love you." When he said those things to me, I knew he meant it. It wasn't puppy love: He wanted to find someone to be with forever. His Mormon family values were too ingrained, and he wasn't savvy enough to understand that I loved my dreams more than I loved him, and would choose them every time.

I knew Meadow would never sign the release. But I also knew that it was the perfect thing to ask my mom, who was eager to get back in my good graces after how badly things had unraveled between us. I called her and pled my case. "You're not doing that, Colton," she said. "This is an adult magazine. It's porn."

"Mom, it's not porn," I said. "When the hell did everybody get so conservative? They all have their clothes on!"

"They're all making out with each other! And touching each other! Colton, you can't do this—you're too young. What if it ruins your whole career?" I didn't understand why she was drawing the line here, after everything I'd seen her do, and vice versa. It felt so shortsighted.

"This is the biggest opportunity I've ever had, Mom."

"What about Abercrombie?"

"Fuck Abercrombie!" It went on like this for several days of phone calls, until finally I wore her down. She signed the release. We scheduled the shoot.

By this point, Jay had moved to Austin, an hour away, and I was spending weekends with him. XY's shoots were always candid and executed on the cheap, and this was no exception: The photographer, who was flying in from California, asked that we meet him at the airport, since he would be staying with Jay. His name was Blane, and he wore a plaid button-down with skate shoes and a Volcom belt. His hair was long, and he was friendly. As soon as we all got in the car, I could feel him warming to me. "Colton, you are just a star," he said. Jay looked irritated; he didn't like anyone else giving me attention, which was sweet in its intentions but also, in this case, annoying—I didn't want him to blow the vibe with the photographer who was going to jump-start my career.

As soon as we got back to Jay's, we began shooting, and Blane wanted to start with my solo shots. I knew exactly what to do. My shirt was off. I changed into the same pair of shredded paint-marked jeans as always. I began lifting dumbbells. I put a beanie on and stuck my tongue out. I looked up at Blane's camera, trying to fuck it, the way I'd seen boys do in previous shoots. I crawled on my knees, changed into a pair of pants that had a hole in the crotch, lay back on the bed shirtless with my legs spread so you could see my white underwear in the rip in my groin. Jay knew that I was a showboat, but he'd never seen me like this. Everything but the camera fell away.

Next, I pulled Jay into the frame. We put oven mitts on and pretended to be baking cookies. We stripped down to our underwear, licked each other's faces, bit each other's lips, sucked on each other's tongues. We went outside to a storage unit and mimed moving boxes, both of us in multicolored tank tops, mine pulled up so it was almost a crop, exposing my pubic hair above the waistband of my jeans. Blane kept positioning Jay so his face was away from the camera, so the focus would be on me. After a while, Jay got cranky.

"Blane, when are we going to do photos of just me?" he said.

"We'll just finish this round and then we'll get you on your own," Blane said. It wasn't that Jay wasn't gorgeous—he was— it was that Jay didn't want to connect with the camera. He didn't love it the way I did, maybe because he didn't need it as badly.

Blane had found out about a party with a bunch of other Myspace twinks that he wanted to go to that night, which excited me, although Jay looked exhausted by the prospect. But he rallied, and we wound up in a hot tub, Blane shooting Jay and me while we kissed passionately, surrounded by a gaggle of lean, muscular boys, splashing in the water.

I liked Blane. He was like David Armstrong in that he didn't seem to want anything from me sexually, which was a relief. But while we were sitting together outside Jay's place, he said those words again. "You're really a star, Colton."

I feigned humility. "You think so?"

He nodded. "Yes."

"I want to go back to New York and model professionally," I said. "I wish I was taller."

"Fuck New York," he said. "Come to L.A. You need to be an actor."

"I think my voice is too gay for that."

"Bullshit," he said. "You can make it in Hollywood. I'll help you." He looked me in the eye. "Why don't you come out to California over spring break? You can stay with me. I'll introduce you to some people." He seemed truly sincere.

"Can I bring Jay?" I said.

"Of course!" Blane said. "You know, Jay is gorgeous too. But you—you're special." I wanted to believe him. It was everything I'd been waiting for someone to say to me. When Blane left, I could tell Jay was relieved. But I was restless. I wanted the magazine to come out, for the world to see me—to see us—for what I was sure we were, bound for something extraordinary.

Los Angeles looked like a dream: the palm trees swaying in the wind against lines of clouds that were dusted through the sky; the long rows of expensive shops that lined Beverly Hills into West Hollywood. And gays, gays everywhere: celebrating their pride, looking free, people laughing and waving, spilling out of gay bars onto Robertson. Blane met us outside a bar called Mickey's, grinning widely, a copy of a glossy magazine in his hand. I grabbed it, and was stunned to see that we weren't just in it. We were on the cover.

"Holy shit," I said, and I stared down at my face. As expected, Jay was tilted away from the camera, in profile, but I was gazing right into the lens, oozing sexuality.

"Congratulations, kid," Blane said. "You ready to meet some people?"

Jay looked anxious again, like this was more than he had bargained for. I watched as he studied the picture on the cover of the magazine. He hadn't expected us to be on the cover; neither had I, but at least this kind of attention was something I wanted. To him, it was a liability.

We went with Blane to dinner at the home of a prominent movie producer who lived in a mansion in the Hollywood Hills. There were other handsome young men there, milling around the cavernous living room; they all looked like me. But the producer didn't sit with us at dinner; he stayed in bed the whole night. When we went into his room to say hello, he was propped up with pillows, and he looked ill. But he had enough life left in him for his eyes to flicker across me, like he was appraising me.

"You boys should come to my premiere tomorrow," he said. "I'll put you on the list." He said it so easily, as if going to a movie premiere was something people just did. Maybe in his world it was.

"He's recovering," Blane whispered to me once we were out of earshot.

"From what?" I asked.

"He got fucked too hard by a guy with a truly massive dick," Blane said. "And it messed up all the nerve endings inside his ass. Now he's addicted to painkillers."

"Jesus," I said. Blane shrugged.

"Want to take his Lambo for a spin around the block?" Blane said. "He doesn't mind."

At dinner, I was seated next to a writer. He was fiftyish and had that familiar hunger in his eyes, like he wanted something from me. "So you're moving out here, right?" he said.

"Yes!" I said. "I'm going to live with Blane and Jay, my boy-friend—he's right over there." I pointed at Jay.

"Ah, young love," he said. "That'll end. When it does, give me a call. I can help you if you need anything." I hated him.

When I got back to Texas, I found out that the writer had somehow gotten my address, and I came home one day to discover a package in the mail. It contained some calling cards—I'd told him I was out of minutes for my cell phone in an effort to avoid talking to him—and a very expensive calculator, because I'd mentioned that I wasn't doing well in math class. It was so strange that they were grooming me, not even waiting until I was eighteen to butter me up, but also it was encouraging: If all I had to do was bat my eyes and flirt with people to get opportunities in Hollywood, that was already what I did all the time. It was the most obvious thing in the world to me.

I could tell Jay was threatened by how people had treated me in Los Angeles, but I also knew that he would do anything to keep me happy, so he gamely went along with the plan to move there after I graduated so I could try to make it in Hollywood. I didn't want him to be miserable, to have to bend to accommodate what I wanted, but I also was convinced we could have it all, together. My last few months of school, getting to L.A. was all I could think about. Blane had sent me home with some copies of XY to give out to my friends. I carried them to school and sold them for fifteen dollars a copy out of my locker, pocketing the money.

My homeroom teacher caught me one day and leafed through the magazine, her eyes widening. "Colton, you really shouldn't be bringing stuff like this to school," she said. "It could get you in a lot of trouble. It's so sexual."

"If anyone has a problem with it, that would be homophobic, wouldn't it?" I said. She eyed me a little anxiously and handed the magazine back to me.

Just before I graduated, I was nominated for prom king. I asked Jay if he would come with me, and he said yes. We rented tuxedos from Men's Wearhouse—my vest was lime green, and his electric blue—and Meadow let us get ready together, probably because she liked Jay and thought he was a good influence on me. At prom, under silver metallic streamers and pink lights, we slow-danced to "I Swear" by All-4-One. I rested my head on his strong chest and felt like his.

I didn't win prom king; that went to one of the football players. But the fact that we were able to dance together, to be together, out in public like that, meant more than a crown.

One Friday at tennis practice, I saw Jay's Monte Carlo pull up in his usual parking spot, just as I was wrapping up. "Your chariot awaits," one of my teammates said, laughing. It had been almost a full school year since the first time he had picked me up there. Running over to his car, drenched in sweat, I slid into his arms like a baseball player sliding into home.

Something was off with him. He seemed as awkward as he had on our first date.

"Is everything okay?" I asked.

"Yeah," he said. "Can we sit in the car for a second? I need to talk to you about something."

"Sure," I said. "But stop acting weird."

The inside of his car was clean, which I noticed instantly; it was always a mess. On the passenger seat was a little black box topped with a white bow.

"Who's this for?" I said.

"Open it," he said, his voice cracking.

"Jay, you didn't have to get me anything. That's so nice. Thank you." I waited for him to put the car in drive, but he kept it off. He knew I was uncomfortable receiving gifts; it always felt impossible to give people the reaction they wanted, like my excitement would always fall short of their expectations. Why was he acting so weird? Obliging, I opened the neatly wrapped gift to find two platinum rings, in two different sizes.

"Will you marry me?" he said.

"What?" I said. "Here? In this parking lot?" But then I saw that there were tears in his eyes, and I realized suddenly that he was serious.

"Will you?" he said again.

I felt like the windows had been blown out of the car. "Yes," I said. "Yes, I will." And I kissed my funny, cute, weird boyfriend and felt something totally pure: happiness.

When I got home, Meadow was there. She saw the ring almost instantly. "What is that?" she said.

"Jay proposed," I said. "We're going to get married."

"Colton," Meadow said, and her voice caught in her throat. "You can't do this."

"Oh my God, Meadow," I said. "This is so predictable. Can't you just be happy for me?"

"It's too soon. You're too young!"

"Oh, *now* I'm too young?" I said. "I've been taking care of myself my entire fucking life, but *this* I'm too young for? Come on, Meadow."

"But—"

"We raised ourselves!" I shouted. Suddenly I was furious at her: for stepping in where my mother had failed, for both the bigness and smallness of it. She'd done so much more than she had to do, and yet, it was so deeply not enough. She had exceeded anyone's expectations as my guardian, and I hated her for that: for not being my mother; for being my mother. "You understand that, right? There's nothing I'm too young for."

"You're going to hurt him, Colton," she said.

I turned away from her. I didn't want to give her the satisfaction of seeing the look on my face, which would have told her everything. That I knew she was right. That I knew Jay was going to end up being collateral damage in my quest to get what I wanted, and it was clear to everyone else that I had no idea what I truly wanted in life. I didn't know what was the matter with me: why I was so hell-bent on chasing this dream. I knew that this thing with Jay wasn't compatible with the life I wanted. But I wasn't ready to let him go.

So I walked away from her, went upstairs to my room, and shut the door, twisting the platinum band on my finger.

8

LOS ANGELES, CALIFORNIA
2007

"Squeal for me, piglet. Want me to feed you your food?"

The voice on the other end of the phone moaned.

"You want to get fat for your master, little piggy?" I said breathily. "You like that? Oink for me now. Tell me how much you love your owner."

The client had called me first to explain what turned him on. In this instance, it was straightforward domination, which I could do, although my strengths were fin-dom—financial domination—and foot fetish. My name on the website was Landon James, which was the name I'd planned on giving my firstborn son, if I ever had kids, which was something I thought about a lot. That name is ruined now, but back then, Landon James was happy to comply.

"I want to be your pig," he'd said in a high, nasal voice.

"That can be arranged," I'd said, dropping my voice down a few octaves so I'd sound as masculine as possible. "Call me back in sixty seconds." Then the games would begin.

I'd signed up for the service thinking it would be a quick way to make some cash and could double as acting practice. Money and experience—the two things I needed most now that I was living in L.A. I'd inhabit different characters and assume roles unlike my-self, and in the meantime, save up enough money to buy a car. As Landon, I could be whatever felt truest in that moment. But most of the guys who called were variations on the same theme. They all just wanted to be obliterated.

One of the foot fetish enthusiasts wanted me to be a giant who wore Timberland work boots, the tan ones with laces. I'd call him a dirty little ant and crush him with my shoes.

"Please don't crush me, sir!" he said.

"You stupid little ant!" I bellowed. "You want me to squash you with my giant boots?"

Just before I'd step on him, I'd tell him I was removing my boots and now I was going to torture him with my smelly socks. After the call was over, I'd mail him my actual used socks and he'd send $300 in cash to my PO box.

My rate had started at a dollar ninety-nine a minute, but soon I'd become so popular that I was up to twenty dollars a minute. The fin-dom guys were the easiest. One of them called me one day just as I was about to get into the shower. I held the phone close to the spigot so he could hear the rushing water. "I was getting ready to take a shower," I said. "Do you really want to inconvenience me? I don't want to talk to you, you piece of shit. This call is getting in the way of my plans."

I heard him panting. "You're going to stay on the line for twenty minutes while I shower and get some stuff done around the house," I said. "And if you're not on the line when I come back begging for my forgiveness, not only will I never take your calls again, I will find you." I could hear the anger in my voice—it was surprisingly convincing.

"Yes, sir," he said, his voice quivering. I made $500 off that call, less my commission to the website.

It wasn't how I'd planned on making it in Hollywood, but it wasn't a bad start—to be eighteen years old, new in town, and making enough cash to pay my bills. I kept my availability turned on all the time so I'd never miss a client, which had me constantly dipping in and out of dinners, shops, or meetings to take my calls. Standing on Santa Monica Boulevard outside a CVS, I'd be cooing into my cell phone: "You want me to fatten you up like livestock getting ready for slaughter?" "Time for your fucking Geritol, old man," I taunted as cars whizzed down the road and passersby eyed me strangely. I could never understand why so many of these guys had such a thing about farm animals, but to each his own. The staff at the local post office got to know me well, since I would make frequent trips to mail off used socks and underwear, which I wore to the gym, then kept in plastic bags so they would get as musky as possible before shipping them off to men all over the country.

Jay didn't seem to mind. He had tried it too, but quit when he found a job that was more stable, working in the kids' club of a gym. I was making more money than he was at his new job, but one of the perks of his was that we both got to work out for free, which took care of one of our few essential expenses. The rest of my money went to the acting classes I had started taking out in Burbank, which were ludicrously expensive: How did it make sense to charge broke actors that much to learn how to act?

We crashed with Blane until one day I was driving down Wilshire just east of Koreatown in Jay's car, which I had borrowed for the day after dropping him off at work, when I passed by a historic building with a giant sign atop it: Los Altos. For some reason, it caught my eye. I pulled over, parked the car, and got out to walk around.

The balconies had green-and-white-striped awnings over them, and the trees lining the cobblestone courtyard were all lit up with amber bulbs strung from branch to branch. In the center, there was a fountain with a statue of a naked woman holding an amphora. Two grand doors guarded the main entrance. Walking into the courtyard felt like being in the middle of a coliseum. I went inside to find a grand lobby littered with antiques: enormous armchairs, sumptuous vases around the perimeter of the room. It looked aged but clean, like old Hollywood—Judy Garland, Bette Davis. Bette had actually lived there years earlier, along with Ava Gardner, Clara Bow, and Douglas Fairbanks. There was a two-story suite that William Randolph Hearst had built for his mistress. But most of all, it reminded me of my mom and the dusty trail where I was raised.

As I was looking around, I heard a voice over my shoulder. "Excuse me, do you need something?" I turned to see a man in a wife-beater and jeans. There was sweat on his forehead; he looked a little animated. I saw him eyeing me in the way that certain men did, and so I pulled my classic scratching-the-V-line-just-above-my-pelvis trick, hoping he'd take the bait.

"Are there any apartments available here?" I said. "I'm new in town. I'm looking for a place for me and my boyfriend." I hit "boyfriend" hard, even though Jay was technically my fiancé, because I wanted him to be clear that I was gay and not available.

"Boyfriend," he said. I nodded. He looked me up and down again. "I do have a unit that's about to be vacant. It's quite small, but it's rent controlled—the current tenant only pays seven-fifty a month." That still sounded like a lot to me, but I smiled.

"That sounds great," I said. "Is that how much it would cost for me too?"

He pursed his lips. "Let me see what I can do."

We moved in a few weeks later at $750 a month.

The building's roof was, to me, the most amazing place in L.A. On a clear day, you could see north to the Hollywood sign and west to the ocean, an unobstructed view. Jay and I would go up and sit under the O in the Altos sign; one of the letters was always blinking. The roof was a junkyard: rusted guard railings painted turquoise, abandoned AC units, a few old chairs people had forgotten and left up there after suntanning, and a cemetery of cigarette butts, mostly mine. My phone rang all the time, dudes on the other end of the line beating it while I told them to eat their slop or else I'd lock them in a cage for the day. But looking up at the stars from that roof, it felt like we were living a Hollywood dream, as glamorous as the silent-film stars who once ruled the silver screen. This was Los Angeles.

The modeling agency hadn't figured out how to market me in L.A. as a short teenage model with dark hair; the look out in California was six feet or taller and blond. I was a fish out of water. Eventually, one of my agents, realizing that I was broke and cobbling together an income doing odd jobs—although mercifully, he knew nothing about the phone sex—asked me if I wanted to drive some of the female models to their castings. It was an easy job: I would pick them up at their model apartments, drive them to and from their bookings, and wait for them if they ran any errands. But I was instructed not to speak to them—not to mention that I was also a model myself, at the same agency, as I was warned it might stress them out if they had to make conversation on the way to a casting.

One morning, I drove a Russian model—willowy and angular, like all of them—to a casting for *Teen Vogue*. As I pulled up, I saw that it wasn't just for female models: Crowded outside was a long line of young men who looked just like me. Why hadn't my agents bothered getting me this casting? As usual, I was going to have to force my way into an opportunity for myself.

After I dropped her off, I parked the car, grabbed my backpack, and retrieved a little bottle of water from the back seat, dribbling it through my hair and tousling it. I grabbed my book—which I always kept with me, just in case—and the boots that I kept in the trunk, the special ones that made me taller. I'd gotten them at a garage sale before my very first modeling trip to New York City. They were dirty and didn't fit perfectly, but they were memorable. Equal parts punk rock and old Hollywood. After pulling them on, I joined the line. There wasn't a sign-in sheet, or anyone monitoring who was coming in and out: As long as you had your book and your comp cards, you were good to go. It was a cattle call.

The editors of the magazine were inside, along with a camera crew shooting a reality show called *The Hills* for MTV; I signed a release on my way in, not even considering that I might end up on

TV. One of them flipped through my book, studying the Abercrombie photos, which had finally come out that winter.

"You know Bruce?" she said. Her name was Lisa Love, and she was the editor of the magazine. A camera crew was trained on us, filming our interaction.

"Yeah," I said. "I worked with him once. Two years ago, when I was in high school."

"We love Bruce," she said. "We work with him often. When did you move to L.A.?"

"Just about a month ago," I said. "I love it here." She smiled.

When I got back to the car, the Russian model was waiting for me outside, looking annoyed. "Sorry—I just ran in to use the bathroom," I lied. She scowled at me and got into the back seat without saying a word.

At the end of the week, when I turned in my time sheets, I got a full dressing-down from one of my agents, who reprimanded me for breaking into a casting. "What the hell is wrong with you, Shackles?" one of them said. They had started calling me that back in New York, both because I was jailbait and because I had a reputation for breaking the rules.

"I'm just trying to work," I said defensively. "I've gotta think outside the box."

"You can think outside the box working as a busboy," he said. "No more driving."

In the lobby of the Los Altos, I was stopped by a short man in his sixties who looked like Colonel Sanders: He had a white beard, round glasses that covered his friendly eyes, and wore a flannel shirt.

"Are you new to the building?" he said curiously.

"Yeah," I said. "I just moved in."

"What brings you to Los Angeles?" he said.

"I came here to model," I said. "And to pursue acting. But I haven't really started yet."

"If you need pictures," he said, "I can take some of you. I'm Jazz. I'm a photographer." When I looked him up online later, I discovered he wasn't just any photographer: He was Paul Jasmin, a legendary artist who was close friends with both Bruce and David, the only other notable photographers I had worked with. His dreamy photos evoked a sensual and glamorous ideal, but stayed firmly rooted in reality. I couldn't take my eyes off these photographs. They captured a universe full of impossibly cool kids living a lifestyle that seemed unapproachably chic, romantic, sexy, dangerous, and dramatic. I loved it.

The next day, I shot with him in his apartment. It was a bohemian paradise—stacks of magazines and books lining the walls, incense and patchouli wafting through the room. "Colton," he said. "I wonder if you might be available next week for another shoot."

"Sure," I said. "I'm always available."

"It's for a magazine called *Teen Vogue*," he said.

I laughed. "Yeah," I said. "I can be there."

The *Teen Vogue* shoot ended up airing in an episode of *The Hills*, in which a bored-looking reality starlet was directed to grab my shoes while another looked off distractedly. Life in L.A. had a funny way of working out like this. For every night spent on the phone listening to a guy jerk off while I told him I would squash him like a cockroach, there would be a moment that was so magical, so surreal, that it felt like a movie. All those plot points lining up just so, coincidences that seemed too good to be true, leading the hero along his journey.

After months of submissions to every acting agent or manager I could find online, I was having doubts. I had made up a fake résumé that said I had done an episode of *House*, a medical drama on FOX. In retrospect, it must have been clear that I was lying, because I wasn't even eligible to join the Screen Actors Guild, but I thought the photographs I'd sent would lure in some interest and help gloss over my lack of experience. Luckily for me, someone took the bait.

"We love your look. We'd like to bring you in for a meeting. See you on Tuesday at 2:00 p.m." That was all the email said, signed by a management company based in Burbank. But to me, it felt like everything—the promise of the future.

I'd finally managed to save up enough money to buy a car, with the help of my first credit card—a $3,200 neon-blue Ford Escort. It was a lemon and it barely ran, but it was enough to get me from place to place. Getting around Los Angeles was exhausting: I could be moving a mile a minute and still getting nowhere, stuck in traffic jams on surface streets, praying that my car wouldn't break down on the 101.

I took the Barham exit and passed the Oakwoods, a famous month-to-month apartment complex where young Hollywood hopefuls and their parents would stay during pilot season without having to sign a long lease. I resented those kids, the ones I saw at my acting classes—protected by the safety net of their parents' money and support. If this didn't work out for me, there was no plan B. Nobody to bail me out.

I parked out front and walked past a green awning into a black box theater. It seated maybe thirty people, and it looked like where you might see an improv show, with proscenium seats leading up to the ceiling. Past the theater was an office, where a young man who looked like a miniature version of me was seated at a desk. He appeared prepubescent, like he was maybe fourteen. I wondered where his parents were.

"Hi!" he said brightly. "I'm Greg!"

"I'm Colton," I said. "I'm here to meet Brad."

"Great!" he said. "He's in a meeting, but you can wait right here."

I sat and waited. On the other side of the lobby, there were two teenage boys roughhousing—they also looked just like me. Through a window, I could see a tiny pool, looking out of place in this depressing courtyard in the valley—but there were two boys in swim trunks swimming in it, laughing. It was so disconcerting to see so many young men who looked like versions of me in Los Angeles. I imagined all of them leaving their hometowns to come here and find that they'd be competing with so many others who looked just like them.

Eventually, I was called upstairs to the office, where Brad was waiting for me with his assistant. Brad was about sixty, wearing a skintight muscle tee and a gleaming white smile of veneers. His hairline looked as if it had been recently rejuvenated.

"How did you find out about us?" he asked.

"I found you online," I said. "I know you represent some of the actors on the WB. I want a career like that."

"Why are you using your hands so much when you talk? And your posture is too . . . loose," he said. "We're definitely going to have to change your mannerisms. They're a little too . . . *theater*."

Code for gay. I stood up a little straighter. "Can you sing?" he asked.

"Sure," I said. I began singing "Home," from the Broadway musical *Beauty and the Beast,* but after a few beats, he stopped me.

"Do you have a new headshot?"

I handed him one of my comp cards from the modeling agency, which was all I had at the time. New headshots cost at least $1,000—money I had saved up from the phone sex line but wouldn't dream of spending on that expense, since I had so many pictures in my modeling book. He studied the comp card. I stood in silence, waiting for him to say something, for what felt like an hour. Did they like me? What were they thinking? Did they respond to my voice, my performance, my look? Suddenly, I didn't want to be there.

"I've seen enough," he said. "You should stay and come to acting class tonight. I'd like to represent you." And that was it. I couldn't believe that was all it took—it felt too easy. And confusing. Was he also our acting coach?

Downstairs, a few actors were gathered by the entrance to the theater, and I realized that they had scheduled the meeting to take place just before the class. I began introducing myself to the other young actors. They weren't friendly. It felt like a room full of mean girls in high school, all the popular kids, the ones who wanted nothing to do with me. Every one of them looked like a star—like they had been *groomed* to be a star. Hair, makeup, clothes. They all appeared to have just stepped off the set of *One Tree Hill.* Ready for cameras, ready for the lights. I was a shaggy-haired kid who looked like he'd just gotten off a Greyhound from Kansas, which, essentially, I had. Modeling, I had so much swagger; I felt like a lion at the top of the food chain. But I had no confidence in my ability to be an actor. Here, I was the prey.

In class, Brad set us up into twos: some pairs of boys, some of girls, others mixed. I was paired with Chris, a good-looking blond boy who I recognized from a teen television show.

"Today you'll be working through the scenes that we'll be putting on in Thursday's class," Brad said. "First, we'll have you cold read on camera."

Chris rolled his eyes. "Sexy scene night," he said.

"What?"

"Thursdays are for sexy scene night," he said with a grimace. I wondered what that meant.

When it came time to read the scene, my hands were shaking. It was from a low-budget film called *The War Boys*, which was about two young men who fall in love while living in a border town. I could hardly get the words out of my mouth, staring at the unfeeling eye of the camera pointed at me.

"Stop moving your face so much!" Brad yelled from a seat in the front row. "Not so musical theater!"

Finally, he stopped me. "You need more practice," he said. "You and Chris take some time over the next couple days to get ready for Thursday's class." Chris looked at me disdainfully. I mouthed "Sorry" to him.

That night, when I got back home, Jay had a celebratory dinner waiting for me. He looked like he'd been waiting for hours, excited to hear about my first big class with my new Hollywood manager. "I'm so proud of you!" he said. "I knew they'd sign you. You were born to do this, Colt."

"My new manager definitely wouldn't agree," I said. "He hated me. So did everyone else." I told myself that their doubt was the fuel I needed to prove them all wrong.

The next day, I met Chris at his apartment in Burbank, where he was rooming with some of Brad's other clients. They all seemed straight, and none of them were particularly interested in befriending me. I was gonna have to butch it up if I had any chance of earning their respect.

As we began reading the scene together, Chris stopped me.

"We're going to have to get really comfortable with each other if we're going to do this during sexy scene night," he said.

"Alright, I'll bite," I said. "What's sexy scene night?"

"We all do sex scenes where we have to get fully naked," he said. "It teaches us how to be comfortable showing our bodies on screen."

"We're doing this scene naked?"

"Yes."

"We're doing a sex scene?"

"We don't actually have sex," he said. "But according to this stage direction"—he flicked through the pages—"I'll be mounting you and thrusting in and out of you. And we have to make out. So why don't we just get this out of the way and make out now? So we're both comfortable." I must have looked confused. "I'm straight. Just so you know." It felt like the setup for a porno.

I nodded. "Okay."

Chris grabbed me by the back of my head and kissed me for longer than I was expecting. Our lips held together; he gazed into my eyes with such tenderness, it confused me. *Were we about to actually have sex? Or was this just method acting?* Then his eyes went cold. "Okay," he said. "Let's run the scene."

On Thursday night, the first scene was with a young actress who was doing Halle Berry's sex scene from *Monster's Ball*. "Make me feel good," she said as tears streamed down her face. She took off her lacy tank top and revealed her breasts.

"I just want you to make me feel good." She hiked up her skirt and pulled her underwear down to her ankles over her stripper heels.

The young actor playing the Billy Bob Thornton part was already on a hit TV show. I watched, paralyzed, as he unbuttoned his pants, stripped down completely naked, and crawled behind her, on his knees.

Mascara tears ran down her face. She stared at us, at Brad. As he took her from behind, she let out a bloodcurdling scream, as if it were real—as if he had just jammed himself inside her. "Make me feel good!" she screamed. "Make me feel good!" It was disturbing: a young woman, being violated while pretending to be violated in front of a class of young actors, for the sake of impressing her manager. These kids had been doing this for years: exposing themselves in front of one another, and in front of Brad. Presenting everything they had for this man. I was terrified knowing Chris and I would be performing next.

We began with our first lines. Eventually, I had to take off my pants. I stared into Chris's eyes, feeling everyone looking at my body. I pulled down my boxers as I got on my knees to turn Chris, bare-naked, toward the audience of the other actors so I could perform a fake oral sex scene on him. That led to him throwing me on all fours and simulating penetration while my dick flapped back and forth, slapping against my stomach. I closed my eyes so I wouldn't have to look at the audience. In all of the things that had happened to me in my life, I had never felt more exposed.

After it was over, we put our clothes back on and stood onstage while Brad critiqued us. "Your balls hang so low," he marveled to Chris.

"Thank you," Chris said.

Then Brad's gaze turned to me. "Colton, we have got to cut that hair," he said. "And please stop moving your forehead so much. It looks like I could grow crops in those lines. We've been over this already."

Later that week, Brad arranged for a hairstylist to meet me at his house in the Hollywood Hills. He presented this opportunity like it was a favor, so I pretended to be grateful as the man sheared my hair military short. Brad had just finished working out with his trainer and there were still beads of sweat on his Botoxed forehead. He balanced a bowl of granola in one hand, a little milk dribbling down his chin, as he appraised my new short hair.

"There's the boy everyone will want to see," he said. "There's the star." I felt naked again. I couldn't hide behind my mop of tween-star hair anymore. And I was going to have to find some way to retrain the muscles in my face so they'd stop moving.

In our next on-camera class, Brad praised me. "Everyone here needs to look at Colton," he said. "This kid is going places." I knew exactly what he was doing: withholding validation, then meting it out one morsel at a time, so you craved that attention even while you hated him for being stingy with it. It was just the kind of behavior that would bond to him the fragile, damaged young people who passed through that theater. I was furious with myself, because I was actually happy he'd said that my performance was strong—like I had passed the test. People with a stronger sense of their own self-worth might have quit after being so humiliated in front of everyone. But I belonged here. I guess I was an actor after all.

"Jay!" I called from the living room. He popped his head out of the bedroom. "I just heard back from John at DNA. They *love* your look."

"Really?" he said. He had a slightly glazed look in his eyes, like he couldn't believe it.

"Yes," I said. "Let's do another quick shoot so we can show them more of you."

Up on the roof, I took digitals of him to send on to DNA. "Tilt your head to the side and squint your eyes," I said, directing him the way all those legends had directed me. "Then look up at me." He focused his gaze on me, laser-sharp, and the light caught his cheekbones just right. "You are so photogenic," I said.

"Look who's talking, Colt," he said. "You say that because you love me."

I did love Jay. I was also growing desperate to get rid of him. Jay was a homebody, domestic, provincial; the more he wanted me with him, the more I wanted to break out and experience the world, and that dynamic had begun to feed on itself, as he leaned in and I pulled away. On weekends, I wanted to go to clubs in Hollywood with my new friends from acting class who had finally accepted me, not to sit on the couch with Jay watching TV like an old married couple. I was still young, and I wanted to experience that. This was the plan that I had concocted: I would get Jay represented as a model in New York, since he had a more editorial, high-fashion look, anyway—he was tall and rangy, six foot two, with an angular face that looked made for the runway and perfect measurements. Then I would end the relationship based on geography instead of the fact that I felt smothered by him—a bloodless death.

"No, you really are that beautiful," I said as I snapped more digitals. For a moment I lost the thread—was I doing this because it was a way to break it off with him cleanly, or because I wanted him to have the opportunity to do something that I could never do, to live the life that I thought I wanted to live? Sometimes I felt like a stage mother: encouraging him to strive, to hustle harder, to be more ambitious, the way I was. Of course I envied him: Life would be so much easier if I wanted the simple things he wanted, if a boy I loved holding my hand and telling me I was beautiful and special felt satisfying. When I looked at him, I wondered what it would feel like to be him. Not to long for notoriety the way I did, not to crave being desired by millions of strangers. To look at our relationship and say, *Yes, this is enough.* Jay didn't care about whether people were thinking about him, as long as *I* was thinking about him, as long as I was close to him. The opposite was true for me: I wanted people to be consumed by thoughts of me, but most of the time I didn't actually want to be touched. I was a vampire, draining the innocence from others to try to get back what I had lost.

Sirens blared on the street below. Jay looked at the camera and his big, blue eyes were full of wonder. They reminded me of the wishing well across from the Arlington Hotel I used to visit when I was a little boy, tossing in a coin and hoping for a better tomorrow. Jay had been shiny as a penny, but he'd lost his luster to me. I only wanted what I couldn't have, and loved people who didn't love me in return. The ease with which he poured his love onto me felt unearned. It was too easy—I wasn't ready to settle down. And I didn't need saving.

Jay signed with DNA, as I knew he would, and went off to New York for a summer of trying to book jobs, the same way I had when I was fifteen. Soon he was sending me pictures of himself hanging out with some of the same models I'd been with in the model apartment, including Eugene, and others who I recognized from magazine covers and billboards but had never met. Even though it was a plan I had engineered myself, I was surprised by how threatened it made me feel. He began working as a driver for a wealthy businessman, and then moved into that man's penthouse with a few other male models. He insisted there was nothing going on between them, but it sure seemed like a sugar daddy situation to me. Nobody knew better than me how wealthy men with power brought in young men like us. I had two secret PO boxes of my own from two suitors in Manhattan, so I knew the drill. When Jay posted pictures of him hanging out with two boys who couldn't have been older than nineteen, who looked just like me, I came untethered. I'd wanted our relationship to end, but I didn't want him to have anyone else either. It was irrational, but it made me furious.

"I know you're fucking one of those guys," I said in the midst of an infuriating text message spree. "I just know you are."

"Colt, you're ridiculous. Are you okay?"

"You're cheating on me, and I know it."

Faster than I'd expected, the dynamic between us began changing. He started DJing at a club called Le Bain in the Meatpacking District, where there were gay foam parties posted to nightlife websites; scrolling through them, I saw Jay shirtless behind the DJ booth. I hardly recognized him. He was skinnier than when he'd left L.A., and although he'd always been toned, now he looked gaunt, dark behind the eyes. I wondered whether he was using drugs. He insisted he wasn't—he was just getting ready to walk in Fashion Week, to go to Paris and Milan. He was going to live out my dream, one that my height had made impossible for me. Eventually, I broke up with him in a text message. Alone in our apartment at the Los Altos, I didn't cry. I steeled myself in the mirror before acting class with Brad. I reminded myself I'd gotten what I wanted: my freedom.

Not long after Jay and I broke up, Brad suggested I start working in his office, where I'd sit behind a desk and submit his clients, my fellow classmates, for television and film roles on Breakdown Express, a casting submission site. He promised that if I did this, he would get me an agent. A few months later, after my best acting class performance to date, Brad called me into his office.

"I think you might be ready to meet with agents," he said. "The one I want to place you with, Chris's agent, isn't interested. Not yet, anyway."

"Okay," I said.

He continued: "Tomorrow, on your lunch break, I want you to leave here and deliver some paperwork I owe him. And you're going to deliver it in a cowboy hat and an unbuttoned Western shirt."

"What?" I said. "Wait, are you serious?"

"Sometimes you have to do things like this to get people's attention in this town, young man," he said. "Now, let's see if you can garner his interest."

Since Brad assured me that this was just what people had to do, I was only a little bit nervous walking into the high-level agency, on Sunset Boulevard, unbuttoning my shirt in the elevator, walking through the packed waiting area, past rows of assistants I thought were fawning over me, but who were in fact laughing at me. My starved abs, all of me just starving for attention. But judging by the look on the agent's face after I interrupted his conference call and delivered him the package, sealed with a devilish smile and then an angelic glance goodbye, I actually thought it might have worked.

The next day, I was over the moon when I was summoned into Brad's office. I thought this might be the moment when he told me I finally had my first agent, that all I'd had to go through the last few months had finally paid off.

"Colton, he still isn't interested," Brad said flatly. "I'm sorry, but this isn't working out. Your voice, your mannerisms—they're still too . . ." He trailed off. Then, finally, he said it. "Gay."

I looked at him incredulously.

"The dialect coach that you've been going to—the Movement for the Actor class you've been taking—the mannerisms class—I just don't think they're working. You still have so much work to do. We think that you will be better served at a different management company."

I sat in stunned silence for a moment. "Are you fucking kidding me?" I said.

He shook his head.

"What am I gonna do?" I asked. Tears trickled down my face. I wiped them away bitterly, furious that this man was making me cry. "I thought I was doing so well," I said. "I thought you all liked me."

"If you're hard up for money," he said, "I know a place that might be able to help." He wrote down something on the back of a business card, then handed it to me. "It's been a pleasure working with you," he said.

Back at Los Altos, I looked at the card Brad had given me. On the back he'd written: rentboy.com. I opened it up in my browser. It was a site for sex workers.

I sat in the silence of my empty apartment, traffic whizzing along Wilshire down below. When my phone rang, I answered it, flattening myself on the bed. I looked up at the ceiling, cradling the phone between my neck and my ear. I felt nothing. I'd found the nullification all these gentlemen callers were looking for, that elusive obliteration, the feeling of being crushed into nonexistence.

"Squeal for me, piglet," I said into the phone. "This is all you are good for."

PART
THREE

9

ATLANTA
2010

The deer came out of nowhere as we turned the corner, the car hugging the curves of the road in the dark Georgia night—I was driving, Holland was in the front seat, Crystal behind us, all three of us wearing beanies and sweaters in the cold. The headlights reflected in the deer's eyes as we approached it, and it froze in the middle of the road, staring directly at us. We were going to hit it. I was sure.

"Colton, look out!" Holland shouted, and I slammed on the brakes so hard the car jerked to a stop, jolting us forward so powerfully that for a moment I thought I'd hit the deer.

"Did I hit it?" I asked. I lowered my arm, which I realized had reflexively risen to protect Holland's chest. She turned to Crystal, shaking her head, then pulled the rosary beads that had hung around the rearview mirror from where they had landed inside the AC vent after our abrupt halt, threading them through her fingers.

"No," Holland said. "I think she got away."

We pulled over to the side of the road, got out of the car, and looked around for a long moment, but the woods were silent. It was so cold we could see our breath in clouds. "I told you to slow down, Colt," Crystal said, punching my shoulder playfully. "Thank God you didn't swerve." We got back into the rental car.

"My hands are always at ten and two," I said. "No broken thumbs as long as I'm behind the wheel." It was the only thing I remembered from my driver's exam.

"Yeah, no broken thumbs," Holland said. "Just faces." She smiled at me. "Close call."

My big moment had finally come. I had booked a legitimate TV show: *Teen Wolf*, MTV's splashy reboot of the iconic '80s franchise. This was the first time it had felt like a sure thing, like I was actually teed up for success.

The week after Brad humiliated me, then dropped me, I began submitting myself for auditions on the breakdowns, using the password that Brad never changed, sending my headshot and résumé from a separate email account. If he wouldn't manage me, I would manage myself until somebody better stepped in.

My first official audition was for a show called *Eli Stone*, which didn't go particularly well in my eyes, but I had feedback from casting in my fake email account by the time I got home. "He really popped right off the screen," it said. "After he gets rid of the nerves, I think this kid has a real shot." Two days later, I swindled my way into an audition for a one-episode guest spot on *CSI: Miami*, and booked it. The day after the episode aired, a call from an unknown number rang through on my cell phone. It was one of the biggest talent management companies in town; they repped some of my idols. How the hell did they get my phone number? After going in for a meeting, they signed me on the spot. The work didn't come immediately, but after a year or two of auditions, I started booking more guest spots, then recurring appearances on TV. Then came *Teen Wolf*.

The team I'd assembled after Brad dropped me always made sure I understood that I was the only thing standing between me and working consistently. "Make sure you stay in character both on and off set," my manager had said to me before I left. It didn't matter who was on my team, the message I got was always the same: *You will not work if you are yourself.* "Look what almost happened, Colton," she said. "The head of MTV almost didn't hire you because of that *XY* photo shoot we've been working our asses off to extinguish. Thank God Jeff fought for you to get that role." Jeff was the creator of *Teen Wolf*, and he had indeed fought for me; I was grateful to him, and eager not to fuck up the opportunity.

I was twenty-two now—more of a man, even if I was playing a high schooler on TV. My demeanor was chipper, but my voice was low, and my mannerisms were on mute. I wore a slight variation of the same wardrobe to all four of my auditions: a checkered flannel shirt under a letterman jacket I found at a thrift store, and high-top Jordans to hide my lifts. I kept that varsity style to help butch myself up a bit. But I had learned the tools I needed to suppress my affect, to make my personality match the way I looked—like a stupid, dumb jock—with just enough silly charm that people would still like me.

And they did like me, my cast mates and the crew. We'd met on the first night we all arrived in Atlanta to start production, and soon we felt so close it was like we were a family—the same way summer-camp friendships hot-wire intimacy. The budget was lean, and the schedule was so tight that most of my scenes needed to be completed in one take so they could spend more of the allotted time on coverage for the two main characters—and rightfully so. Holland and I were the only two out of the six who were hired as recurring characters for the pilot episode—as opposed to series regulars, which we'd become if the show got a full order—to save budget on the show. But even on our off days we'd drive to set and stay there all day just to watch our new chosen family do their thing on camera.

Every potentially bad turn was immediately counterbalanced by something memorable.

Holland had been in one of the *Bring It On* movies, which I had actually auditioned for but didn't book, and much to her dismay, a cheerleader convention descended on our hotel at the same time we were staying there for the pilot, a parade of pom-poms and perfume. Watching her try to maneuver around the hotel without being noticed by them was one of the funniest things I've ever experienced. I wasn't about to let her groundbreaking work in that movie go unnoticed, so I told every cheerleader in sight that a *Bring It On* star was in their midst.

The hair and makeup trailer caught fire—on a day it was empty because we'd been snowed out for work.

I left my phone in a taxi—and the person who got in after

me happened to be a crew member who returned it to me safely—the same day I got the important call that I'd booked my next job.

The theme of our time in Atlanta was being in the right place at the right time. Every second with this crew felt meant to be. Watching each other from video village, seeing the work we all did. Eating biscuits and gravy at breakfast in Midtown after night shoots. Crashing at each other's places like brothers and sisters. Our bond was so immediate that I felt comfortable enough to come out to them, and they promised to keep my secret.

In my memory I am the ringleader, the mother hen of the group: wanting to protect everyone, make dinner reservations, organize hangouts. I loved the glamour of the fact that we were there to make a TV show, but most of all I wanted to show these people who were close to me a good time. I just wanted everyone to like me.

I lived in a studio apartment, which was the first place I'd ever really lived alone, and it felt so grown-up—like I was established, as I put my newly bought wineglasses in the cabinet. My shiny glassware, my shiny glass-walled apartment. Everyone could see inside from the adjacent buildings, but I was only looking into one reflective surface: the mirror.

My appearance was changing, and for the better, I thought. All of us had a trainer who would ensure we were in peak physical condition—all paid for by the network, thank God. My once-skinny frame now had muscle stacked on top of my bones. "You're at five percent," my trainer said after pinching my skin with a caliper to check my body fat.

"I wanna get down to four," I said. All I'd eaten that day was androgen and diuretics. "Am I supposed to feel angry, and like I'm gonna faint?"

"You just need to make sure you stick to your diet and you'll be fine," he said. "No sugar. Don't drink too much water. Two meals a day of just meat and vegetables. And no butter or carbs." That was all fine with me. Little did he know that the bottle or two of Santa Margherita Pinot Grigio I could put away at night was the only thing I wouldn't compromise on.

My newly sculpted body was starting to become a friend, but it was also my arch-nemesis; I hated it even more than I had before. How could I act fake, look fake, not eat, work out twice a day, not drink water, and continue partying? It was all beginning to feel like too much when I discovered the magical pill: Adderall.

"Colton, why do you keep skipping training?" one of my cast mates asked. "And how do you look so toned?"

"It's a new medication I started," I said brightly. "On top of my supplements!"

With Adderall, I could party harder and starve longer. The only problem was that I kept on fainting—everywhere. I'd faint in the bathroom late at night, coming to disoriented in between the sink and the tub, staring at the toilet brush. I couldn't tell anyone for fear of sounding the alarms and having to change my behavior: I only took three secret trips to the emergency room in an ambulance during the first season of the show, which I considered not bad considering how I was punishing my body.

"Maybe you should slow down on the Adderall," Holland said one night. "You're starting to look too thin . . . and you know I don't ever say that."

"Okay, Mom, I'll get right on that. You want a bump?" I said with a smirk, snorting a line of Adderall off the glass table in my glass apartment.

We would hang at the bleached white studio of a famous

music producer, people fucking in a glass-walled recording booth, a variety of drugs splayed out on the table, though I was the only one partaking. Or at Jungle, a warehouse club with neon paint party nights where we would dance topless, sweating and pouring water all over each other and decorating one another's bodies with blue and green paint. It felt like Big Daddy's had, but it was gigantic and bright, not depressing: There were so many beautiful people there, and they weren't just conventionally attractive—it was the joy that radiated from their bodies of being able to be that free, and in the South of all places, all those men and women who had come from all over to be who they wanted to be, in ways that I wasn't brave enough to do yet. I hadn't known that Atlanta was as gay as it was: I'd gone there thinking that it was just some place where you go to work, and instead it was a place to live, to have fun, to experience joy. Dancing on the boxes at Jungle didn't give me the plasticky feeling I had in Los Angeles: The joy on my face was a Technicolor dream.

But best of all was a strip club called Swinging Richard's. Mouthwatering, soul-crushingly beautiful men of all backgrounds, shapes, and sizes. The confidence of these dancers blew my mind; was that what I'd looked like when I was on the go-go box at Big Daddy's? Even at my wildest, probably not. I would snort Adderall in the bathroom and study them until four in the morning, then strut across the room, past the stripper poles and the huge main stage to the VIP section, which cost forty dollars to get inside, but back there, the mood was anything goes—a private dance for a hundred bucks got you fifteen minutes in the back right next to the bathroom and the ATM. As long as that ATM was dispensing cash, I could spend it all there—thousands of dollars.

I wasn't rich. None of us were, working on that show. We had been given a series order of twelve episodes, and my fee was $12,000 an episode—which felt, at first, like a lot of money. But after commissions to my team, taxes, and a $4,000 monthly publicity fee that would begin when the show aired, I was lucky if I had anything left. I could have spent every penny at Swinging Richard's. I was so well known there that when I walked in, the DJ would announce over the mic, "Cody's here!"—or whichever alias I was using at the time. My face always looked the same, but my name tended to change based on how drunk I was at the point of my arrival. And I always wore a baseball cap so I wouldn't be recognizable—to cover my tracks since the show was about to come out.

The dancers would send me free drinks and follow me around, which made me think that they liked me, that they thought I was cool and hot. But now I know they were just like me. They knew I had something they wanted, and they were going to do whatever they needed to do to get that. I had no problem giving them money. It returned me to how I'd been as a teenager, tricking and using my body to get what I wanted. It brought me back to my life before I was in the industry—when I was wholly anonymous, and it didn't matter what people thought about me, where I could just wear a mesh tank top and tube socks up to my knees because I wanted to, because I felt free. I'd traded my authenticity for something I'd thought would be so much better— fame, security—but it turned out I mourned the thing I'd been so eager to give up.

Yes, this was where I belonged: Swinging Richard's. And the longer I was there in Atlanta, the more Swinging Richard's began to feel like home, and soon I was sneaking out of dinners and ditching hangouts with cast mates so I could go sit by myself at my lonely table in the back of the strip club, fantasizing about the men who were grinding away onstage, sipping my vodka–Red Bull. These dancers had freedom, but they wanted to be in my shoes—I knew that.

What they didn't understand was that to be in my position meant being judged on the biggest possible stage. I was too gay to play the lead, and too modelesque to play anything but mean or stupid. I was constantly being told by casting directors, and my team, that my look was too threatening—a term that incensed me. It meant my face would take away from the material, or the other people cast, as if I were a pit bull who needed to be reined in. I wanted desperately to be able to show people the real me, so they could see beyond my features, so they could meet the silly, sensitive big kid I was at my core—but having a career and the ability to live as my true self felt mutually exclusive.

Those dancers I watched—maybe they could eat meals. Maybe they wouldn't have to down bottle after bottle of alcohol to feel normal. Maybe they wouldn't need to take so many pills. Maybe they *were* normal.

I wish I had been able to be more present and appreciate what I had when I was on the show, instead of tirelessly climbing the Hollywood ladder. Dylan, who I nicknamed Pickle, dancing in between takes. Making fun of Holland, always pursing her lips for the camera and secretly videotaping her one-of-a-kind comedy. Crystal cuddling up to me in our warming jackets in the freezing-cold woods at 3:00 a.m. during night shoots. Posey playing his guitar on breaks in my on-set trailer. Hoechlin and me drinking red wine out of the bottle, watching movies on the projector screen he'd set up in his empty living room, sitting on two beanbag chairs and laughing about our personal training sessions together. But what I remember best is sitting in the back of Swinging Richard's, trying to touch something I'd already left behind.

A few months later, the whole cast arrived in New York for a week of press interviews and photo shoots. On my way to the hotel, I asked the driver, who had been hired by the network, whether he could take me through Times Square; I'd been told there were billboards for the show up there. "They want you to see it tomorrow," he said. "I was advised not to take you there until you can all see it together." I thought it was odd, but I didn't mind waiting, at least until I could be with my cast mates so we could have that experience together. The show had premiered that weekend after the MTV Movie Awards; it was the first time in history that MTV had ordered a big scripted show like that, and being out of our Atlanta bubble for the first time, we were about to find out firsthand that the world had already declared it was a smash.

The next morning, we met down in the lobby. It was funny to see everyone together at a fancy Midtown Manhattan hotel, dressed to the nines by stylists and coiffed by glam teams, after we'd been so plain and simple in Atlanta all those months. Nobody acted differently; everybody was normal. We were mostly just excited that we didn't have to pay the bill. It was a sweltering New York day, but the energy of the morning felt like a breeze.

There was a barricaded area for us to make our arrival in Times Square, where we were going to the NASDAQ building to ring the bell. I'd thought we would just walk into the building and it would be easy. But when we exited the car and began walking through the crowd, there were hundreds of people screaming our names, shutting down Times Square. *Tyler! Holland! Colton!* The scale of the crowd was overwhelming—I had never seen anything like it. Holland, in her towering heels and minidress, was walking too slowly, and people were reaching across the gate to try to touch us, even though we were flanked by security guards.

Tyler and I picked her up and carried her through the teeming mass of people, fans screaming, weeping, handing us notes and letters that they had written us. The walk was only a few minutes, but it felt like hours. *Is this what life is like now?* I wondered. *Is this my new normal?*

Now I understood why I hadn't been taken to the billboards. They'd thought it might not be safe for us anymore.

I wanted my family to be with me for the *Teen Wolf* premiere in Los Angeles, but Clinton couldn't come—he was in college back in Kansas—and things with my mom were strained. She wasn't even living very far away, having moved two hours outside L.A. to live with and take care of my grandparents, who'd left Arkansas to be closer to a few family members in California. But the second a drink hit her lips at night, her behavior became too much for me to handle. She called me every day—in the middle of photo shoots, during press junkets and fashion shows—but I always pressed ignore, doing my best to erase my longing for her.

Instead, I flew Summer and Meadow out to Los Angeles and arranged for glam to come get them ready for the big night. I dropped them off at the Beverly Center while I was down the street doing press so they could shop for accessories to match the Hugo

Boss outfits my team had pulled for them, since I had become an ambassador for the brand.

"You didn't have to get all of this for us," Summer said in her thick Arkansas drawl.

"I'm just happy y'all could mosey on down here," I said. "Giddy-up, hookers!"

I was desperate to share this experience with people I loved, wanting to make it everything they'd ever imagined Hollywood life could be. I'd promised them it would be magical, a special occasion they'd never forget, and I thought they'd be excited to come for that reason alone. The day of the premiere, they sat in hair and makeup for hours, getting primped and coiffed, because I wanted them to look and feel like glamorous young Hollywood ingenues. I had never been to an event like this before, one where photographers and reporters would be focusing on me as a star of a show—I didn't know what to expect. We were joking around and I did a practice photo shoot with my digital camera so I could help them with their poses, since I'd imagined they'd be walking with me down the red carpet, all of us arm in arm.

But when we arrived at the Roosevelt Hotel, the red carpet all lit up with flashbulbs and teeming with people, the publicists wouldn't let my sisters walk with me. I looked at them helplessly, their expectant faces that they'd spent hours having painted. I didn't know what to do. "I'm not taking pictures on the carpet unless they take pictures of them as well," I said. A beleaguered network publicist ushered us on with an exasperated sigh.

Reporters and photographers were calling my name, pulling me over, telling my sisters to get out of the way so they could take solo shots of me. Soon they were swept off the carpet so the next cast member could be photographed. I was rushed down the line to do interviews. Panicked, I scanned the room for them, but they weren't in my line of sight. It was chaos.

"Can you look for my sisters?" I asked one of the publicists.

"We have to get you through these interviews," she said. "They'll be fine."

I was worried that I had let them down. But the flashbulbs were so bright, and reporters were calling my name. It felt important.

After two hours of doing press, I had nearly forgotten that my sisters had come with me to the event. Grabbing a drink at one of the bars inside, I was mid-conversation with a top MTV exec when I finally saw them standing alone at a table on the outskirts of the room and made my way over to them.

"I'm so sorry," I said. "I've been looking everywhere for y'all."

"No, you haven't," Meadow said. "We've been watching you milling around the party for an hour."

"This is my job, Meadow!" I said. "It's not my fault no one wanted to take pictures of you." I was upset that I had failed to make the experience what they'd wanted it to be, but I was also angry at their attitudes.

"We didn't even want to take pictures on the red carpet," Summer said. "We just wanted to be with you on your big day."

"Bullshit!" I said. "I had to get all this set up—hair, makeup, styling—just so y'all would feel comfortable being at a Hollywood party!"

"We didn't ask you to do any of this, Colt," Summer said. "You insisted on it. We just wanted you to feel comfortable having us here, so we let you. All we wanted was to be with our baby brother."

That realization stunned me. I had done all this for selfish reasons. I had made my sisters into something they weren't and didn't need to be, ignoring the fact that they didn't feel comfortable with layers of makeup on, cinched into outfits that didn't feel true to who they were. They were real people. They didn't need attention from photographers or network executives. They just wanted to watch me shine. Instead, they had watched the character I had created, sauntering around a party.

Someone from the network tapped me on the shoulder and pulled me away to do one more group cast photo, and as I looked back I caught one last glimpse of them both, arms crossed, looking unhappy. I did this all the time: I promised the world but never came close to delivering what they were expecting.

All three of us were still pouting as we watched the premiere from a cocktail table, in the middle of a hotel lobby that had been blocked off for the event. The opening credits rolled to the sound of cheers and the first episode began to play. It was my first time seeing it on screen, but I couldn't focus on what was playing out in front of me; I was still grappling with my sisters' frustration, and annoyed that somehow it seemed to be all my fault. When I looked back on screen, Tyler, the lead of the show, was walking through the woods. At that moment, a herd of deer galloped through the trees past him, their eyes glinting and bright, and I thought of that night in Atlanta, with Holland and Crystal.

The deer up on screen had the same empty, scared look I had in my eyes in the photos from the red carpet at the premiere. My mouth was smiling, but something was wrong. There was something I was looking past, something I was avoiding. Something I kept trying to swerve off the road to keep from hitting.

10

VANCOUVER
2012

Airplane coffee. A bowl of mixed nuts, uneaten. The worn leather of the seat, the crack of light through the window. The voice of a flight attendant: "And for those passengers on the left side of the plane, you'll see Mount Rainier and Mount Saint Helens . . . the volcanoes of the Pacific Northwest!" She said it with genuine excitement, as if she hadn't already said it on every flight she'd worked. I wondered whether she had been an actor too. At baggage claim, I could hear my mother's voice playing in my head: "Make sure you pack light, or else you'll be waiting an extra thirty minutes for your luggage." She was right, as usual. I felt her with me, guiding me in the right direction, as I arrived to begin work on my new show, *Arrow*.

As I exited baggage claim, I searched for my name in the array of drivers holding signs. Just beyond, there were a few dozen people gathered, waiting. Waiting for me. Motioning for me. It wasn't like any airport paparazzi situation I'd been through before—at least, not on my own. When I was traveling with famous friends, I'd see the same twenty paparazzi and fans waiting, who somehow always knew your exact location—from checking the airport logs online somehow, or getting tipped off. They greeted us with a barrage of white flashes, taking pictures and waving headshots for us to sign. They were as fervent as if they'd been waiting for loved ones to arrive, like we were their family. But here, in Vancouver, I was alone, which meant all these people had come to see only me.

They weren't my family. They didn't know me. Still, it was a strange thing to get used to: the way people recognized you when you didn't recognize them, the look of familiarity in their eyes. Even glancing past the face of a stranger, the look in their eyes might make you stop and wonder: *Wait, have I met this person before?*

I pushed through the crowd, signing a few photos and taking selfies, being friendly. It was winter. Outside, the air was crisp and cold, but the light bearing down on me had never felt so hot, or so close.

I was staying at the Sutton Hotel, which was infamous: It was where they put all the actors when they first came to town, when they were shooting their pilots or their movies, before they moved into apartments of their own.

I was thrilled. Staying in hotels for me always felt a little dangerous. At the time, I was lonely and secretive. The privacy of a hotel room felt like the only place left where there were no limits or boundaries. I would get up to all kinds of bad behavior every time I stayed in a hotel—it seemed like I was always racking up tabs on my credit card, waiting for male visitors to walk into the hotel bar, rejecting those who showed interest, and chasing after those who showed none.

Vancouver was a different city, but I hadn't changed.

It had only been a few weeks since my time on *Teen Wolf* had come to a close. A failed contract negotiation was what the press ran with, but the real truth was that they didn't want to pay me the same amount as everyone else, which wasn't a lot to begin with by Hollywood standards, even though my working quote—the fee I would be paid to appear on anyone else's show—was higher than most of the cast's. It didn't help that I was represented by a team of people who made the *Teen Wolf* production's life a living hell. So in order to get back at my team, the production refused to pay me the standard salary. I was constantly caught in the middle and at the end of the day, the only person who ended up getting hurt in the battle was me. Overnight, I was back to being unemployed, with not even an audition lined up. Fortunately, a producer friend of mine who I met when I first moved to L.A. had called me directly to audition for three episodes on *Arrow*. When he asked me, he had trepidation in his voice, as if he was worried I might say no.

"Are you kidding me?" I said. I was over the moon. "Of course I'll audition!" The next day, after reading two short scenes on the Warner Bros. lot with casting and the producers, I got the call that I'd booked it.

Clinton cried when I told him the news that I was going to be playing Roy Harper. "Are you kidding me?" he yelled. "Roy Harper becomes Red Arrow—then Arsenal! You are gonna be the sidekick, like Robin is to Batman!" I didn't know what he was talking about.

I couldn't have cared less about comics; I had never seen anything superhero-related, and I didn't even own a TV. But *Arrow* was the most watched show in the CW's history—with even more viewers than *Gossip Girl*.

Just as I had in Atlanta, I made friends in Vancouver quickly— not only with my fellow cast mates, but with the stunt crew, hair and makeup people, and entire casts from other shows that were filming in town. I felt lucky to have friendships like this. I didn't see it at the time, but in many ways, they reminded me of my mom at her most loving.

And just like with my mom, I'd pull away and distance myself exactly when I needed them the most. No matter how close my friendships were—no matter how much I felt like I was being seen for who I actually was, as the weird, sensitive, funny guy instead of the guy with the "threatening" face—there was still some part of me that always felt like I was living a double life, that there were pieces of me I couldn't show anyone, publicly or privately. I was out to those closest in my life, but not to the public—I was acting twenty-four hours a day. Outside my family, there was no one in my life who had known me before I'd come to L.A. I'd fallen out of touch with all the friends I'd had in Kansas.

On the weekends, I'd take my rental car down the scenic route to Whistler, the Lions Gate Bridge fading into the distance. The sight of that bridge was enough to make me weep—its limestone-green bars roping together a gorgeous path for travelers to look at the beauty of Vancouver from just outside the city. On one of those drives, traveling through the clouds along the Sea-to-Sky Highway, I stumbled upon Porteau Cove. I wondered where the hell I was as I crossed the weathered train tracks that cut through an expanse of untouched coastline stretching to the horizon. It felt like heaven, water trickling in from nearby falls down into the bay, past timber logs that floated on the arctic-temperature water. The abandoned shipping docks looked like archipelagos, shades of aqua rippling from the calm sea into cascades of evergreen trees. I would drive to a long breakwater that jutted out into the sea, lie on my back, and stare up at the sky, smoking, thinking, remembering. Feeling sorry for myself, for reasons that I couldn't explain. Once I got to Whistler, I'd get a massage at the Scandinavian spa, and then I'd get fucked up on Maker's Mark whiskey and wander through the village alone without worrying about running into people who knew me.

But in Vancouver, I began rarely leaving the house I'd moved into after being asked to join the show full-time as a series regular. To me, the city started to feel unwelcoming; people seemed even lonelier than I was. It was almost always cloudy. Over time, I'd become agoraphobic—afraid of the world and everybody in it, including my own friends. Wherever I went, I felt like I was being watched, or judged. I only went out to go to work, get more booze from the liquor store, or grab an occasional coffee and sandwich to suppress the hunger gnawing at me from the inside out.

Things are different when you become famous. More different still when you are taking pills all the time. You become less present; life gets a little blurrier. There were long days on set, but I don't remember them. I can't recall many of the high highs or low lows, even though I know they happened. Instead, what feels most vivid is the memory of the constant loneliness.

***

What happened to me? I wondered. I begged friends and family to come visit me, planning champagne brunches, spa weekends, waterfall visits, birthday parties I'd host in a friend's luxurious cabin. There was a five-star restaurant with an igloo inside, and cross-country ski trails where Meadow flew off the side of a mountain and almost ended up in the lake. But I was miserable. I would get home from work in the evening, drink wine, watch drug documentaries, or disappear into a YouTube rabbit hole. Hours later, I'd wake up, completely alert from the amount of sugar in the alcohol I'd consumed, but also somehow numb. My hands and feet would feel like ice. At first, I thought it was the climate, but when I read more about the stimulants I'd been abusing, like Adderall, I learned that they caused blood flow to move toward the heart, causing numbness in the extremities. I would lie down and when I got back up, the day would already have disappeared.

Of course, I was there to work, and I was working. Not just working—according to the millions of followers I was accruing on social media, I was famous. I was in *GQ,* on the covers of magazines, sitting front row at Fashion Week, and flying on private jets. I was being treated well, and the show was a hit; my career didn't fizzle after leaving *Teen Wolf* and I had bounced back stronger. But I was miserable. The beautiful house I was renting felt like a prison.

On one of my days off, my mind was racing and my loneliness was at a peak when I stumbled upon a YouTube video about tantric healing—a sexual practice of hands-on bodywork with a teacher that was meant to help ease trauma and increase sensitivity, connection, and emotion. When I was having sex, I was always too busy obsessing about myself, trying to give the other person the version of me I thought they wanted—Instagram Colton—or just wanting it to be over. I wondered whether tantra could help me be more present during sex. I found a local tantric healer named Thomas and in his photos, his eyes looked alive, like they could start fire. Looking at his pictures, I wanted my insides to burn. I wanted flames licking at any walls I'd built inside myself.

He lived just across the bridge in a modern concrete building. When he opened the door to his home, wearing a white tank top and cargo shorts, and led me into a comfortable room with beanbag pillows, bohemian rugs, and overstuffed couches, with candles lit, I knew I would be safe there. He instructed me to take off my clothes and sit cross-legged on the ground in front of an altar. Then he undressed and sat directly in front of me, knee to knee. He grasped my hands, which were cold from the lack of circulation and always a little sweaty.

"Look at me," he said. I met his gaze. His eyes were ships in my ocean. I tore my gaze away. "No," he said. "Don't break eye contact." I met his gaze again. "Eye contact is our primary source of intimacy," he said. "It's the main practice that people don't bring into sex, even though it's the most important thing to forge connections between people."

Suddenly it occurred to me that he could see the darkness that lived inside me, whatever devious energy I was always trying to keep at bay. *I'm not ready to let that go*, I thought. It was in my chemical makeup, that badness; it was the thing that made me myself. What if he could see it? What if he knew that my Adderall had kicked in? What if he knew I was a fraud? What if he knew that I was there only to feel something momentarily, with no intention of learning how to change? As I continued staring into his enormous, incandescent eyes, I wondered if he could see that loneliness.

Eventually, he had me lie down on a massage table, where he checked my chakras, running his hands all over my body as electricity built inside me. When his fingers grazed the nape of my neck, I felt like a marionette, as if I would move left if he were to guide me in that direction. It felt as though if he had flicked his wrist just once, I would have levitated off the table. When he turned me over, I was hard, and pre-cum had leaked out onto my groin, but I didn't feel dirty, the way I normally did during sex.

He pressed on areas that he thought might need releasing. I squirmed the most when he arrived at my stomach, beginning to feel faint. "This is where you carry your anxiety, right?" he said. I nodded. "Look at me," he said. I opened my eyes while he pressed on my belly and kept that sustained eye contact for as long as I could. But I knew he couldn't heal me. There was something too deep inside me, something I couldn't get out no matter what I did.

After another sleepless night of scrolling the loneliness away, I broke down and decided to hire some company. I couldn't go out to the gay bars; I was too well known now, and still closeted, and already too drunk on my problems to handle another sip.

"Hi, I'm Cody," I wrote. "Any chance you might have avail tonight for an hour massage? Sorry for the last min." The text was to a couple I'd found on a massage website. I'd frequented massage parlors when the loneliness was too agonizing, but I needed something more than that now: the warmth of breath on the back of my neck, kisses between my shoulder blades. *Destroy me, put me back together, push me out into the winter night.*

"Hi, Cody! We can definitely make tonight work! Are you looking for just one of us or both? Our four-handed massage rates are well worth the money, and well worth your time." His name was Luke and he was a square-jawed hulk.

I showered, sprayed on too much cologne, wrapped myself in a trench coat and two oversized scarves, and put on black fingerless leather gloves and a pair of black combat boots that I called my bedlam boots—a uniform for chaos. Waiting outside their building, about to press a fingertip to the silver call box, I had the thought: *You don't have to do this. Go be like everyone else. Go out to a bar. Meet people.* The door opened and a stranger stepped past me, looking at me funny—did he recognize me? Or was he just confused as to why I was standing out in the freezing cold? I stepped inside.

I caught my reflection in the mirrored elevator—my stupid Jimmy Neutron hair, stiff with pomade. If only I felt as secure as my hair did.

Luke was shirtless, twelve feet tall, a chiseled Ken doll with a crew cut. When he hugged me, I was reminded of camping—when the air mattress would rupture and deflate in the middle of the night and I'd wake up with my face pressed against hard rocks on the ground. He was prehistoric, craggy as a rock face. His husband, Joe, was tall too, with a tattoo of a sun around his navel, one ray traveling south to the strap of his Andrew Christian briefs.

"Hey, papi," Joe said, his hands caressing my lower back.

"You want a drink?" Luke asked.

It was the fantasy I had imagined come to life. I felt like a twelve-ounce porterhouse, medium-rare and still bloody, plated to perfection. I wanted to be devoured. Never mind that they had a "Live, Laugh, Love" sticker magnet and a pile of self-help books on the table, depressingly. I just wanted the moment to stay sexy.

And for a few hours, it did. Luke wedging his hand between the waistband of my jeans and the small of my back. The music turned up. Joe's fingertips tracing my goose bumps. They were tender. I looked from one back to the other, my eyes tattling on my body, telling the truth about what I really wanted. To be made whole. To feel good. To be safe. To be seen for what I really was—emotional, sensitive, broken. Maybe it was easy to accept love. Maybe I'd just been waiting for these two.

I thought about them all week, a tape playing in my head as I sat alone having dinner at Bin 941, a tiny eight-table restaurant where I ate almost every night of the week, slugging back old-fashioneds and lying to the same waitress that I was waiting for a friend. I scrolled through their photos obsessively. What a perfect couple they were. I made up stories about their backgrounds, and the lives they must have lived. I was too afraid to text them again: What if the reality of another encounter ruined the fantasy? It was better that they lived only in my mind.

One night I went to a local bathhouse. After tilting my baseball cap down and paying my entrance fee, I changed into the white towel that I always fastened above my belly button, the better to hide any extra fat I was convinced I had. The night was shades of red, black, and blue. Everything was wet. Moans rang through the hallways like an alarm. Porn played on TV screens overhead. I loved this darkness—it was exciting, wrong, taboo. Through an open doorway was Joe, lying on a cot.

I said his name without thinking about it and he looked up.

"Do I know you?" he said. He scratched his skin idly. His eyes were dark. He was strung out.

"No," I lied. "My bad. I thought you were someone I know." I couldn't believe he'd forgotten me, that he didn't even recognize me.

"Are you looking?" he said. "I could really use some extra cash."

I went up to the locker where my wallet was stored, grabbed all the money I had, and walked back down the hallway. By the time I got back, the door was closed, and there were loud sounds coming from inside. I slipped the money under the door and left.

When I looked back on the site where I'd found them, they had individual profiles. I made up a story that they had split up. Joe had relapsed. Luke had tried to forgive him so many times but just couldn't make this work again.

But the truth was, I didn't know them. They had been masking something dark. They were just like me.

11

PARIS
2014

Things were getting blurrier, from the pills and the lights, but I remember Paris.

My schedule was overflowing with events when Julie reached out again. I didn't want her to call; it was distracting. I saw the call come in, let it go to voicemail, and took another Adderall. I was supposed to be having a moment. She was reality crashing in, exactly when I least wanted that.

I was running around New York then. It was December and the city was strung up in lights. When the right pills were in my body I lit up like a Christmas tree too. I was leaving a club, and there were paparazzi there, and everyone I was with was also on TV, which made

the whole thing feel like a TV show, but one that I was living, instead
of acting in, although maybe I was always acting even when there
weren't any cameras rolling, but we stepped out of the door and off
went the flashing lights of the paparazzi as beautiful person after beautiful person stumbled into the back of black cars, and as the car door
pulled shut I couldn't hear the street noise anymore, just the vibrating
of my phone, Julie dialing me, wanting to hear my voice. Wanting to
remind me that her house was one I could always call home.

In the car next to me, the guy I was secretly dating saw me
looking at my phone. "What is it?" he said.

"Julie," I said.

He shook his head. His mouth puckered. He always looked a
little jaundiced. His attitude was constantly sour. "You're not going,"
he said. "We're going to Miami for New Year's." Every year a few of
us were paid to have our pictures taken at a hotel in South Beach.
I flashed back to last year. The pulsating of a synth beat in some
nightclub, everyone wearing white. A dancer reclining on the lap of
a director most would kill to work with.

"I have to," I said, and I looked at the phone again.

"She only cares now because you're famous," he said. He didn't
know my family, but I let him believe he was right.

For years, I had known about her, this branch on our family tree I
had been too afraid to climb. Julie was my half-sister on my father's
side. But right when I was ready to meet her, I was reminded that
she was going to die. She had stage four melanoma, and the doctors
weren't sure how long she'd live. However long that was, I knew
it wouldn't be enough for us to build a relationship, and so I had
avoided her attempts to connect.

I don't know why I suddenly knew this was the right moment to go, but I did. I packed my suitcase and left the fancy hotel. Meadow was waiting for me downstairs, in a rental car, and we rushed across town to grab lunch with my half-brother Joshua, who shared a father with Julie and me and had helped facilitate this meeting. I'd first met Joshua when I was six, at the house with the den, because my dad was trying to be a good father, but that didn't last long; he sent Joshua back to live with his mother in a matter of weeks.

We drove out of the city, into the snow. Although it was Christmas, nobody was feeling festive. I was carsick. I was always carsick. I was emotional. I was always emotional. Knowing I was about to meet an extension of my father for the first time only made me feel worse.

Julie taught special education at a high school in Vermont. She was prim and proper. Her world was almost as small as she was. This was all I really knew about her, what I'd gathered from the brief conversations we'd had on the phone when she would call me and I would sometimes answer, sometimes not, because it felt like too much.

But when we pulled up at her house in Vermont and she hugged me for the first time, she felt like family. She felt like mine. She was eighty pounds. Not eating was just making her sicker. Our eating disorders were on the list of possible things we could bond over. She had pale, freckled skin and fiery red hair, like the flame of a candle.

All night, she told stories about her dad, who was my dad, and all the times he had fucked over both of our moms, and how bad that felt, but it felt good to talk about it, to hear her stories and know that they had the same tortured man at the center of them.

She showed me her vision board, which had pictures of cities she'd never been to. She dreamed of Paris. She had cut out a photograph of the Eiffel Tower. She had been to New York, since it was only a few hours away, but she hadn't seen the world that I had seen. Anorexia was taking everything that the cancer hadn't already devoured, and I was afraid that she wouldn't get to see much more before she was gone.

It was the only way I could reach out and touch my father—to have a relationship with Julie. Even though we both detested him, he was the thing that bound us together.

Maybe I was trying to make up for lost time. Maybe it was just one of those moments that happen in life from time to time when you know what the right thing to do is and you just do it, instead of making up excuses. It seemed like every day somebody wanted to give me an opportunity, to do some kind of sponsored job or show up at an event, and within a few months of meeting Julie, an offer came in to go to Paris for a Comic-Con appearance, and I knew Julie had to come with me. I called her husband and told him that both of them were meeting me in Paris. He said no—it was too much. I insisted. Then I called Clinton to tell him he'd be coming too. It's funny how you can be so many different things at once. I was young and I was famous and for those reasons and so many others I was the worst, but I am also proud that I did at least that one thing right.

Clinton and I stayed at a friend's place so Julie and her husband could have the nice hotel room. We rented golf carts and took a tour of Versailles, all of us dressed up like we were in a runway show, even though we were just sitting in the sun all day.

I'd bought Julie a vintage Chanel jacket at a used clothing store and she hugged it around her thin frame like it was the most precious thing she'd ever worn. She was talking in a fake British accent, doing some impression of Marie Antoinette she must have seen in a movie. We were such tourists. It didn't matter. That was my family. My boyfriend kept calling me and I kept declining the calls.

It was midnight at the Eiffel Tower when the lights went up, and the lights were the same orange as Julie's hair, and we stood there in silence. Even the buskers stood still to soak in the moment. She had tears in her eyes. It was as if I were seeing it for the first time too, this big, bright world that I'd gotten to bask in. I tried to see it as she did. We were together, this family, broken as we were. She was grateful for the beauty of it, and so was I. She had to sit down on the lawn. She was tired. But she was very much alive. When I think of that night in Paris, and the expression on her face, and the tears in her eyes, I don't feel sad. I think about how bright the night was, and how, for a split second, everything was full of light.

12

LOS ANGELES
2016

I pressed out a cigarette into an ashtray. My vision went sharp, then blurry. Adderall, then liquor.

"Cheers!" I said to my two friends who were gathered on the front porch of the house where I lived. The Seattle Seahawks were winning on the TV inside, but I was drowning myself in cheap wine on the porch, the way I always did.

"To the Dead Dads Club!" my friends said in unison. They were like little brothers to me. We drank together often. All our fathers were deceased, which gave us the perfect excuse to drown our sorrows without looking like we had a problem. They actually didn't, but I knew I did.

Who were these boys? They were years younger than me, both pursuing careers in photography and fashion, always decked from head to toe in Fear of God and John Elliott, rarely worried what anyone thought about them, never thinking to wipe the cigarette ash from their sleeves, always broke, but they had enough to buy beer, so who cared? They were Seattle-born, artsy, tattooed, skateboard-riding straight boys, enjoying the California life. I was jealous of them.

"You guys are so hip," I said.

"Okay, Dad." They laughed. It was a nickname I had earned after years of telling endless corny dad jokes. Sometimes I felt like the old man you'd see in the movies running out on the front lawn, waving the newspaper in his hand, yelling at those pesky teens who'd ride by on their Mongoose bicycles, a friend perched on the back wheel pegs. Always recounting the days of my youth.

"What I would give to be twenty-five right now and not famous," I said. I gulped back some Two Buck Chuck and swatted away a fly.

"What I would give to be twenty-five, rich, and on TV," one of them said.

"I'm not on TV anymore," I said, and I wasn't. I had walked away from my full-time job on *Arrow* at the beginning of the year, supposedly because my contract had ended, but it was really because I was too depressed and I couldn't stand working with one of my cast mates. My mental health was deteriorating rapidly. I felt like a house in the middle of a flood—something tired and decaying. Besides, I was making more money from paid social media posts than I had made on the show. Of course, being on the show had helped legitimize my brand, but my busy publicity schedule and constant self-promotion on social media was what kept the deals coming in. It had even helped me book a big studio movie. Yet there I was, drunk on the front porch of a rental house, feeling used up.

After saying goodbye to my Dead Dads Club buddies, I stumbled through the front door past my roommates and best friends, Ally and Trav. Ally and I met shortly after I booked my first job in L.A. I had interrupted her in the waiting room at an audition for an episode of a short-lived show on the CW and said a great big Kansas hello to her. She was so confused as to why I was talking to her that she got up and continued practicing on the other side of the room. A few days later, after I booked the job, I excitedly climbed into the hair-and-makeup trailer, and there she was too. I said hello again, she rolled her eyes, and we had been friend-married ever since. When Trav came into the picture a few years later, I had to open up our relationship.

They were watching the game on the couch, but they looked up worriedly as I fumbled for the fridge. The noises of bottles rattling was a sign that would always prompt them to come check on me.

"Hey, Colt," Ally said. "You okay?"

"I think the boys drank most of my wine," I said. *Where was the fucking corkscrew?* I opened the silverware drawer and used a butter knife to push the cork in.

"Here, Colt, let me help you," Trav said.

"I don't need your help," I slurred. "I can do it on my own."

I felt them watching me manhandle the bottle, the cork that was about to sink into it. "All I want is one more glass of wine," I cried, and as I did, steadying my hands around the knife and giving it a deeper push, the cork shot to the bottom, and red wine spewed out all onto the walls and ceiling.

Thinking nothing of it, I grabbed a shirt from the adjacent laundry room, ran it under the sink, and swung it at the ceiling, trying to clean the wine from it.

"Colt, we just painted the walls and now we're gonna have to paint the ceiling," one of them said. I looked at them, worry on their faces—and annoyance that was long owed me after the hundreds of failed attempts on my part to take their feelings into consideration and respect their belongings, so many excuses, and all-around terrible roommate etiquette. Suddenly I was humiliated. I brushed past them and locked myself in my room.

Drunk that night, I had reached my breaking point. I was so tired of clinging to the belief that everything was going to turn out alright. That the depression would go away. That the anxiety would pass. That my heart would heal. That I wouldn't think I was unlovable forever. That I would get through these feelings of emptiness the way I'd persevered through my upbringing and made it in this crazy town. I opened my computer, searched "fancy rehab in Malibu celebrities go to," and dialed the number for the cliffside treatment center I knew was favored by starlets.

A friendly operator answered. "Aw, baby, you don't have to suffer alone," she said. "I promise you made the right call." Her tone assured me that she meant it.

After an hour of talking to her on the phone, my voice drunk with desperation, she took my credit card number and set a pickup time for later that day, where a driver would deliver me to the treatment staff. I imagined paparazzi pictures capturing me with my face covered in designer sunglasses, my publicist issuing a public statement on my behalf. I would eat yellowtail sashimi from Nobu and argue with them about which rag mag would get the exclusive photos.

A few hours later, I woke up from my dream and checked my credit card statement, which had a new charge for $57,500. *Fuck.* I also had an email from the Four Seasons Miramar, with a confirmation for the bungalow I had reserved. Why had I booked myself a stay in rehab and then immediately booked a room at a fancy hotel? Had it been buyer's remorse?

I threw some clothes I found on the floor into a suitcase and rushed out the door past my roommates' bedroom. My car sailing down the 101, I argued with myself about what to do. I wasn't ready for rehab, was I? Had things really gotten that bad?

At the Miramar, I brushed past the perfectly manicured shrubbery along the coastline and hauled my things into the bungalow. An old, rustic wrought-iron light fixture hung above an aged dinner table with a rusted bucket in the middle, couches upholstered in beige stripes, and vintage picture frames that looked like the ones I hoarded from garage sales and kept in my garage. I tossed my duffel bag onto the floor and ordered room service.

Why was everyone so happy there? Was it the rolling breeze delivering scents of honeydew and sweet tobacco, the perfectly baked French fries that resolved all my hangover problems? In reality, it was a feeling that only money could buy, something I'd been fortunate to have but too quick to rid myself of. After finding my spot on a daybed, I took deep breaths and sunned myself for an hour or so, my eyes flicking between the bougainvillea and memes on my phone. *Raise your hand if you've ever been personally victimized by tequila.* I laughed as I bit the end of my cocktail straw. It wasn't time yet.

I replied to the email from the care coordinator at the rehab, explaining that my concerns had been premature and I didn't actually need to go to rehab. All I'd needed was a change of scenery.

At a restaurant on Third Street, a few minutes from the Grove, a mall where I'd go if I needed extra attention from the paparazzi who waited under the movie theater marquee across from the fountain—"Here's my card, call me if you ever want to tip us off"—I went to dinner with friends.

"Colt, are you dating anyone?" one of them asked.

"Oh, you know me," I said. "Eternally single. Maybe I need to move to the woods." I dropped my voice an octave in case anyone was listening. "Maybe then I'll be able to find a giant man who will club me over the head and claim me as his property."

Moments later, our server approached the table. "Hi, I'm Brant, and I'll be your server this evening," he said. "Would you like to start with an appetizer? Our oysters pair nicely with our signature mignonette sauce." It was like I'd just discovered Sasquatch. He was six foot six, cocky and burly, a muscular beefcake. I made eyes at him all through the meal, too intimidated to make a move, but he barely seemed to notice me.

After we finished, when I was at the valet, he approached me. "Were you really gonna leave without saying goodbye?" he said.

"You didn't look at me once the entire night," I said.

"And you couldn't take your eyes off me," he said. He wasn't wrong. I gave him my number. A few days later, he texted. "Meet me at Norm's on La Cienega at 7pm," it said.

I arrived early, practicing lines I thought I would use on him in order to match his confidence and sexy appeal. I could do that ably when I was around most gay men, but not around this type—the kind of guy you'd let lock you in a trunk as long as he promised not to drive it into a nearby lake. Tall, barbaric, and covered in tattoos—that was my kink.

He got there thirty minutes late, rolling in on a beat-up Harley and greeting me with a hug and no acknowledgment of his being late. Over dinner, he talked about how his dream was to move to Thailand because he had a thing for Asian guys, his brushes with the law, and the annoyance of drug tests from his parole officer. I was smitten.

After getting irritated with the waitress for asking to take a picture with me, he said, "Let's get outta here." In my head, that meant going back to his place. But when we got outside, he gave me an awkward hug, put his helmet on, and rode off down La Cienega. On the drive home, I felt embarrassed that I was attracted to men like this, and humiliated that they would never give me what I wanted.

The next morning, I woke up to a text from him, expecting it to say that I wasn't his type, or that he didn't date actors—a common refrain in Los Angeles—but instead it was an invitation. "You mentioned you weren't doing anything today, so come over. Be ready. And I don't like any body hair, FYI." A normal person would have been repelled by this fuckery, but in a flash I was in the shower with a razor and shaving cream in hand.

I pulled up to his apartment building in East Hollywood and he met me on the street. "Let's go upstairs," he said.

The apartment was derelict, with stained walls and a mini-fridge plugged in next to his mattress and box spring on the floor. A parakeet flew out of the bathroom and landed on his shoulder. "This is Pickles," he said. He handed me a towel. "Shower," he said. It was like he was testing me to try to uncover if I had any boundaries at all, and I didn't. I gave him a look that said, "Game on," stripped off my clothes, and jumped into the shower. Pickles watched from atop the shower curtain. When I walked out in my towel, Brant looked at me rudely. "I didn't tell you to come out yet," he said. Wordlessly, I went back into the bathroom and sat on the edge of the tub. I wasn't sure what he was going to do to me. I wasn't sure if I cared.

Over the course of that next week, I waited by the phone until Brant was ready to use me. I'd come over and get him off while he laid a taser on the dresser, which he threatened to use on me if I didn't comply. Eventually, the taser was replaced with a gun.

After the first week, he asked me to rent us hotel rooms, where the scenes would get more gruesome. The sex was painful and loud, the bed knocking against the wall like an intruder breaking into the house. He had gauze bandages on his shins that I figured were covering up staph infections, but I didn't care. Slaps to the face, hands blocking my air flow, tears flowing down my face as he took the condom off midway through and shoved it in my mouth. I only cried because I wanted him to see the tears, so he could feel like he was in control, which he was.

Driving home, I felt nothing, empty, obliterated, the way the men I talked to on phone sex lines as a teenager had wanted to feel. I understood them now. There was something wrong, deeply wrong. And I knew what it was. Being in the closet made living a double life acceptable. I spent all my time in such a big lie that all the other little lies felt unimportant somehow—what was one more? My identity was divided, and I was crumbling.

———

One night, I met my old agent and a friend of his for dinner at a glitzy steakhouse in Beverly Hills. The friend was an Oscar-nominated screenwriter, and he was gay too. I began explaining to him how I felt like I was buckling under the weight of the closet, that I needed to go public with my sexuality. He cut me off.

"Don't do it," he said. I'd heard this before—from my team and nearly everyone else I encountered in the industry. I'd been urged to stay in the closet for years. I was told my career would suffer if I came out. "It's not just about your image," he said, digging his knife into a slab of red meat. "It's the mystique. You're an actor, right? The audience already has all these suspicions, these assumptions they've made about you. They don't want anybody to tell them they're wrong. But they also don't want to find out that they're right."

Why was it that night that I snapped? I felt belittled and patronized. It was humiliating enough that my team had spent years sending cease-and-desist letters to everyone who posted my *XY* shoot. I was angry—angry about my personal life being encroached upon, angry about being told what to do. When I saw a camera, I smiled. I was always fixing my hair, checking my reflection, trying to look picture-perfect just as long as I could, swerving any indication that there was something feminine or gay about me. And I was tired: tired of lying about who I was.

"Thanks for the advice," I said. "Go fuck yourself." I stood up and threw my credit card at him and stalked off.

On the curb outside, there were paparazzi. Someone on my team had probably called and tipped them off. Somewhere along the way, these people who took commissions out of my checks had decided that they owned me, and I'd let them, because I was scared of what would happen if I lost them.

My doctor, Gary, looked up at me from his notes after one of my frequent checkups. "This sickness you're describing," he said. "Do you think it's due to the fact that you're still holding in your sexuality?"

I was surprised by how audacious the question was, even coming from my doctor of almost ten years. He looked right at me, right through me.

I nodded. He was right. It was time, I told him. I knew I had to come out.

"Do you know how you're going to do that?" he said softly. My mind went blank. *How?* I had never gotten this far. On the precipice of it, I had no idea what to do.

I couldn't say what had brought me in to see the doctor that particular day: It could have been my agoraphobia, my depression, my anxiety, an ambient fear that the world was taking my life away from me. Arranged dates with starlets for the paparazzi, no access to my bank accounts, having to ask permission to leave town—even if only for the weekend. The weight of knowing I had a secret, the same secret I'd been carrying my entire career, from Los Angeles to New York to Atlanta to Vancouver and back again. Somewhere along the road, that secret had taken over my life. It didn't matter how wide my smile was—it was all an act. I was sick and tired of acting. It was suffocating me. It was why I had sex with people like Brant. It was why I drank. It had to be.

I stared at the blank wall across from me for a little while before I started to cry. In that little doctor's office on Robertson and Wilshire, I wept. He told me that it was all going to be okay, but I don't think I believed him.

"I have another patient coming in a few minutes," the doctor said. *Wrap it up, Colton*, I thought, blinking through tears and sucking in the sterilized, antiseptic air of the examination room. I tried to dry my eyes, clear my throat, and stand up tall. Already, I could feel it all coming back, burrowing deeper into me—that thing I couldn't bring myself to put words to but that I knew was the source of all the pain that I had come here in the hopes of fixing.

I guess it'll have to wait, I thought. A twinge of regret shivered down my spine. As if I couldn't wait any longer. As if I hadn't waited long enough already.

"I think my next patient is someone who can help you. Just hold tight for a moment," he said. That was all I needed to hear.

A few minutes later, I shuffled into a different exam room. Walking felt like such a chore, I could barely carry my body anymore, the weight of all my problems. Staring at the ticking clock, waiting for that door to open until the glint of the metal doorknob faded into the corners of my peripheral vision like the wing mirrors of a car, keeping one eye behind me as I traveled down some road to nowhere, I wondered what would happen if I fell asleep right there on that table.

The patient who walked in was a publicist who represented several openly gay actors. We shook hands.

"You doing okay, kiddo?" he said. "Gary told me you're having a hard time with things. Do you want to talk about it?" He already knew who I was.

"I need to come out for my sanity," I said, starting to cry again. "Do you have any advice?"

"Don't worry," he said. "I'm going to take care of all this for you. Come to my office next week and we'll set everything up. You're in good hands."

In his Hollywood office, he already had a game plan prepared.

"I think you're at a point in your career where you can do this," he said. "The press knows you. We don't need to introduce you to the world. You don't need a big *Out* magazine thing. Not for the initial announcement. We mention it in a piece of press that's set in a way of framing this as your next chapter—a new beginning." I nodded numbly. This was long overdue.

When the article came out, I was in Paris for another superhero convention. I'd brought my friend Kevin along. Kevin was a manager, but unlike most people I knew in the industry, he was actually trustworthy; I knew he would be a vault with my secrets. He was an absolute ham and the ultimate hype man. I upgraded us to a suite so we could dance on the balcony overlooking the Eiffel Tower, recite monologues from funny movies—anything to keep me in high spirits during this emotional time. The morning I knew it was going to be released, I sat outside as the sun came up, wrapped tightly in a white hotel robe. I hadn't told anyone besides a handful of my closest friends that I was going to do this. I couldn't deal with that part—anticipating what everyone would say. My team had told me for so many years that it would ruin my career. I was afraid I was about to prove them right.

The article went live—an interview with *Entertainment Weekly*. It was wedged into a paragraph partway through the story: "Haynes, who is in fact gay but has never publicly addressed his sexuality . . ." I stared at the words. It was hard to believe it was real.

Within the first ten minutes, I was deluged with text messages. Tweets. Posts to Instagram from famous people. Emails from agents and producers. I was the top global trending topic on Twitter for that entire day. There were messages from every actor I'd ever met. Every designer I'd ever been photographed wearing. Best friends. Total strangers. All gathering together and writing the most gorgeous, beautiful things on social media to show support. It felt like all the love, all the support, all the promise in the world flowed through me that day.

Maybe this really would fix everything. Maybe I shouldn't have waited so long.

Kevin and I danced on the balcony and drank champagne as the sun went down, and I felt whole for the first time in what seemed like forever.

***

Within a few weeks, the endorsements that had been keeping me afloat financially dried up.

"I don't know what to tell you, Colt," my branding agent said on the phone. "The *EW* article was a great moment, but we're just having a hard time with these contracts." He paused. "We did get one incoming—do you know an app called Grindr? They're interested in having you be the face of their new product, Gaymoji."

I hung up the phone and looked around my house.

I texted Brant.

I poured myself another drink.

13

LOMA LINDA, CALIFORNIA
2018

I was in seventh grade the first time I thought my mother had died. After knocking on her bedroom door for what felt like an hour, I walked around back to check on her through the window. She was lying facedown in her unmade bed, fully clothed in Levi's and a suede fringe jacket in the dead of summer.

I panicked and started yelling. "Mom, are you okay?" I climbed through her window. When I reached her bedside, she was still breathing, but she didn't come to until the next morning.

I never asked her if she'd been able to hear me that day. If she was just too exhausted from the life we were all trying to survive. If she just wanted to be done with it all, the daily struggle of trying to put food on the table, or to get a second away from the children who resented her, who called her a bitch or a drunk on the regular. The children who made sure she knew what a fuck-up we thought she was.

That was what was ringing through my mind when we gathered at Loma Linda Medical Center on a beautiful spring day in 2018. An exasperated nurse was standing in the hallway.

"Hello, everyone," she said. "So many people coming to visit Dana! Which one of you called about getting her a new room?"

"I did," Meadow said. "Hi. I'm Meadow."

"That's an unusual name," the nurse said, friendly.

"Thanks," Meadow said coldly.

"Let me see what I can do," the nurse said, taking the hint that this wasn't the time for small talk.

We formed a circle around my mother's hospital bed, leaving room on the side of the machines she was hooked up to so the doctors would have space to tend to her. The nurse side-eyed us.

"I'm sorry, but we can't have all of you crowding her," she said. "We need space to check on her and there's already too many people in this room."

They were words she would immediately regret. I looked to Summer, then Meadow, then Clinton, then to my cousin Amanda. We were like a pack of rabid wolves, rage bleeding out of our eyes, ready to rip this woman apart. When one of us was hurting, we'd do anything to protect each other. We were never afraid to walk into a fight and never knew when to stop.

It was the first time all of us had been together in a long time, and it looked like we were having a party in my mom's hospital room. It was against policy to sleep in the hospital, but we weren't going to leave unless someone physically removed us.

I had cemented myself in one of the leather recliners at the foot of her bed, wearing a flannel shirt, a pair of black Gucci slides that smelled like dog shit and never stayed on my sweat-drenched soles, and some black denim jeans that I couldn't button anymore. I had two water bottles, one on each side of me—one was filled with Ketel One, the other with Patrón Silver. Options, just in case. I'd take a swig the moment I opened my eyes. I never left the house without them.

The doctor entered the room in a white lab coat. He'd treated my mom for her alcoholism multiple times in the past. He'd taken biopsies, done procedures to stop her internal bleeding, treated her for ulcers and complications from cirrhosis of the liver.

"I'm so sorry to have to deliver this news to you," he said, "but she has six months left. If she's lucky." The room became airless. "I've warned her many times. Dana's known about her declining health for a while now. I don't know if there's much more we can do for her."

I looked at my mom. Her eyes were pleading.

Dana. Dan Dan the Mustard Man. My everything. My mama. My undiscovered silent-film ingenue with a devastating, Marlboro-stained smile and an eye roll so potent you'd forget the entire plot. Style so effortless that you'd have no idea this devil wore Payless. A rare breed. Lassie, Cujo—that bitch. Always sleeping with a knife under her pillow. One smoky eye on us, one on the door.

When one of us got sick, we all got sick. As kids, when the stomach flu came around, she always let us have the only bathroom in the house while she threw up in the kitchen sink.

Now, it made sense. When she got sick, we all got sick. I wished I could give her my life, my blood, any strength I had left after drowning myself in alcohol and pills right in front of her while she was dying from the very same disease.

I tried not to remember, but the memories all came flooding back that day, watching her sleep in her hospital bed with her gigantic Dollar Tree sunglasses, hooked up to six machines filtering new blood through her.

She heard that I was going to get married before I had the chance to tell her myself. Somebody in the family had told her. She called me, bawling her eyes out on the phone, telling me that I was about to make the worst mistake of my life for getting married too soon. But I didn't listen to her. Instead, I just offered to have an Uber pick her up and bring her to Los Angeles so she could meet her future son-in-law.

When she arrived at our house, she came spilling out of the car in a pink negligee with her cirrhosis stomach hanging out, her pants unbuttoned because she was too big to fit into them. She didn't care. She was sobbing. The driver had to help her walk up the long hill.

That night, she went on a bender—yelling, crying, trying to break things in the house and begging us to find a man to come fuck her. "I'm dying!" she slurred. "Get a man over here right now to fuck me one last time." Eventually, I got her into bed and made her a cocktail with two Ambien in it, then made another when the first one didn't work. Still, she stayed awake, hollering the entire night.

The next morning was Mother's Day. I was so furious with her that I packed up all of her things and put them in my car before she woke up. I left out a couple of outfits for her to choose from for the car ride. But I wasn't about to let her cause any more damage to the house, or ruin her last chance at being invited to our wedding. While I drove, she tearfully pleaded with me to talk to her, to look at her. I did neither. When we arrived, I tossed her luggage on the curb in front of her trailer and didn't even say goodbye.

The weekend of the wedding, which took place in Palm Springs, she was on her best behavior, but still needed to get a little mischief in somehow. There was a man at the Parker who would ride around on a bicycle, delivering juice to all the guests lounging around the pool. My mother was wearing her white Daisy Dukes and flip-flops and her purple blouse with her signature dollar-store sunglasses when she stole the bike and tried to ride off with it. Her hair was dyed bleach blond, a hint of gray showing through. Everyone laughed when they heard what she had done.

She'd mentioned that she didn't want to wear anything fancy, so I drove her to a small thrift store on the outskirts of town. "I just want to feel beautiful. And I want to feel like me."

I knew that all that would take was a dress from a thrift store and some hair spray. The last thing she wanted was to be around all these famous people, many of whom knew all the stories about her I had told them, but who didn't really know her, and who she didn't know at all. But she looked like the most famous person there. She was wearing a black dress that had a black sequined half cardigan that almost looked like a cape to cover her shoulders, in case it got cold. A friend of ours who owned a jewelry shop in Beverly Hills was attending the wedding and loaned her a small fortune in diamonds, but even without them, she would have looked the part of a legendary movie-star-gorgeous model, shining brighter than the spotlights all across the Parker. She had brought a picture of her favorite character from *To Wong Foo*. She wanted to look exactly like Vida. The second hair and makeup began, she started crying and didn't stop until the ceremony was over.

She loved me more than anything in the world. I knew that, seeing the glimmer of tears in her eyes reflect off mine in the moonlight above one million red roses as we walked down the aisle.

She knew that the marriage was going to end before it had even begun.

A conference room, somewhere in mid-city. A lawyer at the other end of the table looked at me, inscrutable behind his designer eyeglasses.

"You understand one of the terms of this divorce agreement is that you may not discuss, publish, or post any information about your ex-husband in any media?" she said. "Without limitation and in any manner. This is a binding nondisclosure and confidentiality agreement."

I nodded and scribbled my signature on the dotted line. Then I leaned back in my chair and stared off at nothing. All I could think about was my mother, dying.

"Colton," the lawyer said. "Are you alright?"

"Yeah," I said. I stood up. "I need a drink."

I went directly to the Waldorf Astoria on Wilshire, checked into a room, and didn't open the blinds once for seven days. When the news broke about my split, text messages poured in, but my friend

Kathy Griffin was the first to demand to know where I was so she could come be by my side. She had seen her fair share of public hardships; she knew that I shouldn't be alone.

I slept through her arrival. When I woke up, she had sent me pictures of her posing with the hotel security guards, who wouldn't let her up to my room without my permission.

I did have friends who loved me; I just wouldn't let them in.

As my mom was dying, I refused to get in a car unless I was driving. I'd blast sad music to make everyone cry, just so I wouldn't feel alone. Staring off into the distance at blank skies and ominous mountaintops, I drove my family around drunk. I demanded control of other people's lives because I had no control over my mother's, and judging by the stench of alcohol on my breath, clearly no control of my own.

In the hospital, I'd hold her hand while she slept. "You're not a bitch," I'd say to her. "You're not any of those things I said you were. You're the greatest person I've ever known." I never got a chance to ask her if she heard me talking to her those nights.

But I also prayed that she was too far gone to smell the alcohol on my breath as I blamed her for all my problems, even as she lay there on her deathbed. *You didn't do this to me, Mama,* I wish I'd said. *I did it to myself. I know that.*

I was making her mistakes, over and over again. I didn't know how not to. The apple never fell far from the tree.

I tried everything I could to erase the sight of her in her hospital bed, filling my head with memories of her playing on a loop.

I remembered creeping into her bedroom when she and my dad were asleep.

"Mama, can we cuddle?" I'd whisper as I woke her up in the middle of the night. "Will you ticki me?" "Ticki" was our family word for running your fingernails lightly across the body. She'd pull me in gently and say, "Lou Lou, don't wake your dad up. We can't make a habit of this." Then, I was older and had to stop crawling in to cuddle with her, except to check if she was still breathing.

I remembered the Red Rock Inn on the weekends she'd bring me to work with her, the room service job she got in Wichita after getting fired from the Little Bear. We'd laugh on our rides to work about all the times I'd delivered food to the rooms, so nervous I'd forget to ask for payment. I'd return to the kitchen where she was preparing the orders and have no money to put in the register, so she'd make me go back to the guests and tell them I made a mistake. I couldn't have been older than twelve, but she risked her job again and again to make sure she spent enough time with me.

Our family had a reputation as the troublemakers in town, but I was pretty sure it was just the other mothers disguising their envy as contempt. Every kid thought my mom was the coolest person they'd ever met. We all wished we could be as strong and independent as her. Even as she longed for a man to rescue us, she knew she could survive without one.

"Chad, I know there's alcohol in those water bottles," she slurred. "You really need to watch out because I've told you this for years—alcoholism runs in our family." Her speech was garbled as she spoke, this time from the medication and exhaustion, not from intoxication.

Chad. The name she called me every day for the last two months of her life. She knew it irritated the fuck out of me, since she remembered everyone else's name. She wouldn't be herself if she wasn't pulling some kind of joke on me.

"How are you doing, sweetheart?" asked the hospice nurse who was looking after my mom at home. She wasn't the only one worried about me—my siblings and friends were too.

"You aren't answering your phone, Colt," a text read. "Everyone's worried about you." Get-well-soon cards poured in from everyone I knew.

My mom was a sleeping beauty dwarfed by her big bad wolves, while her little piglets lay awake in the adjoining room, preparing to let her go.

I still wear a pair of her socks, wondering what it must have been like to walk in her shoes, trying to log the miles that she never got to walk.

After three months of watching her fight for her life, we gathered around in a prayer circle with a local priest to send her spirit to heaven, before my cousin Amanda was instructed to stop sponge-feeding her water. Amanda had taken leave from her job as an occupational therapist in Colorado to make sure my mom was comfortable the last few months of her life. She had trained as a healer; her energy was nurturing and witchy. The care she showed my mom was a debt I knew we would never be able to repay.

Now, standing with the priest, it felt absurd that we were all praying for my mom to let go peacefully. We weren't a churchgoing family. After her prognosis, I used to pray to God to keep her alive, and now he was taking her when I needed her the most.

I took a day trip back to Los Angeles with Summer, her husband, and kids in an attempt to keep our sanity. I planned a whole day: I had arranged to bring them on the Warner Bros. lot for a tour. I'd never taken the tour before, but I knew I couldn't tolerate the planned version, so I just had a friend put our names on the list so we could get past security and sneak into the *Friends* exhibit, the museum, and any other place that let us in. I was so drunk and miserable I could barely function. After the tour, we went to Santa Monica to play arcade games and ride the little roller coaster.

Shortly after we got off the coaster, my phone rang. It was Amanda. "Colty," she cried. "I think she's passing. I think it's happening." We had already had months of watching her die, but I needed to be there with her. We raced back to her home in Hemet, two hours away, in our separate cars, every red light torturing me.

She was already gone when I got to her bedside. I stayed with her for an hour, holding on to her. And for that hour, I was her little boy again, hand-rolling cigarettes for her again, helping her pick out her outfit for the day. Taking photographs of her in her curlers and silky nightgown. Inhaling her secondhand smoke. Walking into the Dusty Trail, the place that we called home, over and over again.

Soon she was cold. We styled her hair in a tight chignon, the way she used to wear it when she worked at the Arlington. Her arms were crossed over her skinny frame. She was covered in flower petals.

14

LOS ANGELES
2018

Mirrors lined every room in the house from floor to ceiling, even by the pool. I couldn't escape myself if I tried. I was dressed in oversized sweat shorts with an elastic waistband. My gut spilled over the top. I stared at the person in the mirror who I hadn't been able to recognize for a year. I had gained fifty pounds. Strangers in the comments of my social media called me "fat Channing Tatum." Tabloid headlines announced that I was being "bashed for weight gain." I didn't care.

I went from room to room, cabinet to cabinet, looking for any bottle I could find, anything left that hadn't been confiscated by the people who had come over to visit me.

A psychiatrist to the stars whose claim to fame was putting high-profile people in psych wards would show up at my house unannounced. I found out later that his visits were being scheduled by my manager. The psychiatrist was his cousin.

"Have you been drinking?" he'd say.

"Yes," I replied.

"Why?"

"Because I want to. Because I can."

Every room in the house spun. I made my way out of the lacquered double doors and onto my front lawn, with its view overlooking Los Angeles. On the three clear days a week, you could see the ocean. I sat on the circular, green lawn in a basket chair, chainsmoking from dusk until dawn, often falling asleep in it. I used to hike Runyon Canyon or work out with a trainer. Now I just woke up and searched for the bottle of alcohol I kept in bed with me, or on the nightstand. I wasn't able to shower that often, because I couldn't walk. I pissed the bed.

I had gotten to this point of paralysis a few times before and was always able to lie and blame it on my anxiety and depression. That lie didn't work anymore. Neither did the dead parents excuse. My mom had been dead for six months now and, as everyone kept telling me, I had to get back to living. But I didn't want to do that. I just wanted to drink.

One morning, my phone rang over and over again. It was my manager. "Colton, production called," he said. "They need you to fly to Vancouver tomorrow to shoot—they've added you into the next episode." I had forgotten that I had signed on to do *Arrow* again.

"I'm sorry," I slurred. "You're gonna have to tell them I'm sick. I can't get out of bed."

He tutted. "They aren't going to be happy," he said. "And they'll have to send a doctor. You okay with that?" The physician would be courtesy of Warner Bros.—standard protocol for an actor dropping out of production and costing the studio a lot of money for having to change locations and schedules around.

"That's fine," I said. It took me hours, but I did my best to freshen up, changing out of my sweats, gagging up repeatedly in the sink from trying to brush my teeth. I was planning to play up the idea that I was sick, but by the time the doctor arrived, I was coughing nonstop from the exertion of having to put myself together.

"You have walking pneumonia," the doctor said. "Let me draw some blood and notify production."

Hours later, my manager called. My blood work had come back—and they'd tested my blood alcohol level. *Fuck.* "Production's going to give you a few episodes off in case you need more time to . . ." He trailed off. "Get better."

"What the fuck does that mean?" I said. "*Get better?*" How passive-aggressive. I was furious. I knocked myself out with Don Julio Blanco to punish them all.

The next day, my friend Kevin came over. He looked at me worriedly. "I'm not telling you what to do, Colt," he said. "But it kills me watching you do this to yourself. I love you too much to let you self-destruct. If you don't agree to get help, you're going to get fired off your show." I grunted in acknowledgment. "I found a detox in Pasadena—all you have to do is get in the car with me. I'll check you in and make sure everything goes smoothly. Okay?" I looked at his face and something opened up inside me.

"Fine," I said. "I'll go."

After a carsick drive through the hills and down the freeway into the valley, we pulled up outside an institutional building. A nurse brought a wheelchair and loaded me awkwardly into it. The lights were harsh overhead.

Inside, I undressed in front of a nurse, and I caught him looking at my body. "Where did you get those bruises from?" he asked. So much of my body was black and blue.

"I've had a hard time walking," I said. "And I fall a lot." It was true.

"You don't have to lie," he said. "If someone is hurting you, you can tell us."

"Nobody's hurting me," I said. *Except myself.* He looked at me skeptically.

"We're going to have to perform a cavity search while we finish the rest of your psychiatric evaluation."

"Why are you doing a psych eval?" I said. I looked around. "Is this, like, a mental hospital?" A million paranoid images flashed through my brain, a *One Flew Over the Cuckoo's Nest* nightmare. The nurse came closer to me and I swatted him away. "Don't touch me!" I said. I screamed for Kevin.

Outside in the hallway, I heard them arguing. Finally, Kevin stormed back into the room. "They're convinced that you're being abused," he exclaimed.

"Get me the fuck out of here!" I yelled. I made my way to the floor as Kevin helped me get dressed. He wheeled me out of the exam room and into the parking lot. As we whirled down the hallways, I turned back, screaming at him. "You tried to have me fucking committed?" I shrieked.

"I thought it was just a rehab!" he yelled. "I swear—I just wanted to help you."

The car ride home was like being in a hall of funhouse mirrors: lights ricocheting in every direction, every brake check feeling like we were about to be hit by oncoming traffic, like I was going to fly through the front windshield from where I was doubled over in the back seat, clutching my distended stomach. Back at my house, Kevin tucked me into bed. I reached for the hidden liquor bottle and secret stash of Xanax in the drawer in my nightstand and swallowed it all.

I woke up from a stupor and lurched out of bed. It was daylight— I didn't know how long I'd been in bed. I stared at my reflection. Mirrors, mirrors, everywhere. The house was beautiful, and mostly glass, with stunning views, but I had never gotten around to buying furniture. Someone had described me that way once—as a beautiful house with no furniture. I had laughed, but it stung. I wasn't a beautiful house anymore. My face was bloated, my eyes slits in my reddened face. None of my clothes fit. I was a punch line, a joke. And what a relief it was that the world finally saw me the way I saw myself.

I was so drunk. I was drunk and seven and my uncle was unbuttoning the fly of his tight Levi's to press my little-boy hand onto his cock. I was drunk and fourteen and Damon was pushing his cock into me for the first time, the first time that this had happened in my whole life, and I didn't want him to hear the pain that was coming out my mouth so I faked something else, like a moan of joy or passion so he wouldn't stop, because I knew that if he thought he was hurting me it would remind him that what he was doing was wrong, and it was also illegal, so while he inserted himself into me I did my best not to let him see the tears. I was drunk and fifteen and dancing at Big Daddy's and a man was saying lick it up, lick it all up, don't miss a drop, keep going, dance, baby, dance for Daddy, keep the dicks hard, keep the men hard, the best receptacles carry the most trash. I was drunk and nobody was listening because who the fuck wants to listen to a pretty person complaining, especially when I knew the only thing I was good for was the way that I looked, that even if I had more than that to give, it was the only thing any of the men wanted, and what was I supposed to do, reply to all the people on social media who had grown up in functional households with stable parents who affirmed and nurtured them, and went on to college, and got normal jobs and normal partners and normal lives, and try to explain to them that while they had the luxury of using their words to hide behind their insecurity I'd spent my whole life selling my body to get attention because it was the only thing people wanted me for, that nobody wanted to hear me be funny, nobody wanted to hear me speak, they just wanted to get me naked and leave, like Uncle Tommy did, Tommy who took my innocence from me when I was six and then went back to Las Vegas and had the audacity to up and die of AIDS before I ever got to tell him thank you, I hate you, how could you do that to me? I was drunk and trying to figure out how to resolve the childhood I never worked through in real time, trying to figure out how a kid like me could get anywhere without keeping everyone's dicks hard. I was drunk and starving myself and never sleeping and dreaming I had been born in a different body, even though the one that I had spent my whole life using to get what I wanted was the only thing I had. I was drunk and there were fans who only cared about me whenever I was looking hot and skinny, who would say that I had changed when I didn't want to stop and take pictures with them at the airport or outside the hotel the same week I got divorced, or the same week my mom died, now indebted to the fame that I'd fought so hard to create. I was drunk and reading comments from gay men on the internet, people I had never met, calling me a fat washed-up divorced flop, perpetuating the lie about how I was the only gay who worked in Hollywood, even though I was barely able to get one job after coming out, and couldn't even get an audition anymore. I was drunk and there were reporters asking me questions about my personal life, adding more nails in my coffin. I was drunk and thinking about the friend who had said, "Come on, Colton, you know the reason you got the job was because the casting director wanted to fuck you," and I knew he was right, but what he didn't see was the expiration date that was stamped on my back like a tramp stamp, the expiration date everyone could see while they were fucking me but I could never crane my neck around to read. I was drunk and stupid because I'd thought coming out would fix everything, and it hadn't, because the real problem wasn't that I was a closet case, it was something much deeper and darker, something terrible and unfixable that everybody else could see. I was drunk and alone and my mom was never coming back. I was drunk and too fat, too skinny, too successful, too washed up, too pretty, too threatening, too short, too honest, too gay, too straight, too cocky, too serious, too goofy, too this, too that.

I was drunk and it was my piñata. It was my birthday party. It was my fucking piñata.

Wasn't this the perfect ending to my story? The way I looked had always been my value. My beauty was a black hole that sucked everything into it. Now, finally, it had collapsed onto itself, leaving only an ugly, ragged remnant behind—a torn place where something used to be. Nobody wanted to sleep with me anymore.

That realization shot through me, and for a split second, I felt free.

I opened my eyes and looked down at my wrist. There was a white hospital bracelet on it, which read Bruce Stark. That was the alias my friends gave the hospital—a mix between Bruce Banner and Tony Stark. They must have given my name as that to keep the press from finding out. Ironic. I'd never felt less superheroic.

I felt a papery hospital gown around my body. Fluffy yellow socks on my feet. Around my ankle was a cord that was plugged into something. I had to pee. As I tried to slip out of bed, the cord detached and an alarm trilled rudely through the room. A nurse shuffled in.

"Nice to see you're awake," she said. "But you can't get out of bed—you can't walk."

"I have to pee," I said. *Where was I?*

"You have a catheter," she said helpfully.

"Right," I said. There was a tube coming out of my dick. Another one coming out of my arm, connected to an IV line.

"You're going to be just fine," she said. "You've had quite a few visitors, you know."

The thought of friends seeing me like this made me ashamed. "That's nice," I said. I closed my eyes and dropped back out.

After a week at Cedars, I still couldn't walk. A doctor told me that I'd taken a near-lethal dose of Xanax on my final bender, of which I had no recollection; it didn't sound like something I would do, but I had to admit that I didn't recognize the person I'd turned into. I had no idea what his intentions were.

On the tenth day, my nurse came in. "Mr. Haynes, there's someone here to see you," she said. She was joined by a woman with kind eyes. They were so big and open, she looked like an alien.

"Hi, Colton," she said. "Do you mind if I call you by your first name?"

I shook my head. She smiled. "I'm Lisa. I work for the Betty Ford Clinic. We help people get into recovery."

I didn't think to question her, not even for a second. I didn't put up a fight like I'd done before when someone had implied that I had a problem. She showed me a pamphlet with photos of the facility and told me about people she'd helped. "I've been sober for over twenty years," she said. "Now my life is about helping other people get onto the path that I'm on."

I told her about how upset it made me when people got angry at me because I couldn't stop drinking. It wasn't my fault, I said, that I didn't know how to stop.

She smiled. "Alcoholism is the only disease you get yelled at for having," she said.

I swallowed. "I don't know if I'm worth getting sober for," I said. "I feel so worthless." She gave me a puzzled look.

"I had a lovely conversation with a few of your friends who just left," she said. "They told me how much you've done for them and how much they want you to be happy."

"I feel like a failure," I said.

"Just because you think things are true doesn't make them facts," she said. "But it won't feel that way forever. I promise." For whatever reason, I believed her.

A Mercedes pulled up to the curb, where I sat in my wheelchair outside Cedars. A reassuring hand grasped my shoulder—Lisa. She wheeled me down the side ramp as I stared at the Emergency Room signage. I was wearing the same cheap sunglasses my mom had been wearing in the hospital.

"Can I take your bag, sir?" the driver said. I shook my head. The car was dark green—my mom's favorite color. It was another little sign that made me feel like she was pointing me in the right direction.

"Easy does it," Lisa said. "Remember what I told you—you need to be your biggest supporter." She helped me into the car and hugged me goodbye.

"Are you sure you don't want me to take your bag?" the driver said, motioning toward the messenger bag that I had slung over my shoulder.

"No," I said. "I'm fine. I'm fine." That small bag was the only thing I had. Inside it was a handful of my favorite photographs; a white plastic bag with the two journals I'd purchased at the hospital gift shop, one black and one pink; and a blue velvet box containing an orange-speckled blown-glass heart, which carried my mom's ashes.

Betty Ford looked just like the pictures, clouds rolling in over the mountains. I carried a handbook that said Together We Will Overcome Addiction on the cover—a little too cheerfully, I thought. I started in detox, because detoxing from the amount of benzodiazepines I'd been taking was a long and difficult process. My temporary room in detox turned out to be less impressive than the lobby; it looked like a motel room in an Econo Lodge, cheap and dated. A nurse searched my bag. I flinched when he opened the box containing the ashes. Then he left my belongings on the floor for me to pick up.

I watched a woman with a short blond bob sitting by the phone in the common room, which was littered with magazines and books and board games, dialing any number she could remember, but nobody was answering. She looked like a housewife. She left messages on every answering machine. "Hi, it's Susan, I'm in a bind—please answer," she said. "I'll call you back in one minute."

"Can I use the phone really quick?" I asked her. I had some phone numbers of friends written down in my notebook, since I knew I wouldn't have access to my cell phone.

"Sorry," she said. "You'll have to wait your turn."

When I finally got to use the phone, I called every friend I could. "You gotta get me the fuck out of here," I said in my voicemails. "I don't feel safe." But I knew it was futile. Anybody who knew me would hear in my voice that I was being dramatic. The realization that I would have to stay here for thirty days set in.

"Aren't you that guy from *Teen Wolf*?" Ryan asked me. He was another patient, sort of a man-child, twentysomething and energetic, and my housemate in McCallum Hall. We were tacking the photos I'd brought from inside my messenger bag up on the corkboard in my room in the residential wing, after finally being released from detox.

"I was," I said. "Now I'm on a superhero show called *Arrow*."

"I hate superheroes," he said. "Want me to show you around?"

I nodded. At this point, I was just grateful to have a friend.

"This is where we have guided meditation every morning at 9:00 a.m.," he said, pointing to an open space in the common room. "That's where we play water volleyball during physical fitness hours." He pointed to a pool, which I could see through the window. His enthusiasm and knowledge of the place made it seem like he'd been there for weeks. "Oopsie daisy," he said, tripping over his untied Yeezys. "I'm still waiting for my boat shoes to arrive. Amazon tracking says any day now. So, you getting cameled tonight?"

"What's that?" I said.

"Initiation ceremony for new guys to the house," he said, looking at me like I was an idiot for not knowing.

"What happens?" I asked.

"You'll see," he said, winking.

After that evening's chores, all the men in the house gathered in a circle in the common area. Nick was the "granny" of the house—the leader, who was selected every week by the staff. "Colton," he said, "if you can pass this test, you can stay in the house. Step into the middle of the circle and get on your knees."

I sighed. This was too familiar. But I got on my knees and closed my eyes as instructed.

"The camel each day goes twice to his knees," Nick said. "He picks up his load with the greatest of ease. He walks through the day with his head held high. And stays for that day . . . *completely dry*." After what felt like an eternity, I heard his voice again. "Open your eyes."

I opened them to see the smiling faces of men gathered around me, cheering and laughing. They picked me up off the ground. I understood that it was just a test of trust—seeing if I was willing to be vulnerable.

"I thought you were going to piss on me, you jerks," I said, laughing. Nick fastened an enamel pin in the shape of a camel to my hoodie.

Now that I was initiated into the house, I was instructed to pay it forward and go pick up another patient named Sam from detox who was moving into our house, the way Ryan had with me. I couldn't wait to play up the whole "Camel" bit. I waited outside detox for over an hour and finally knocked on my new housemate's room. This timeline wasn't working for the pranks I had planned, but the sight of him was no joking matter. Sam was the kind of fragile soul you'd stop on the sidewalk to help—eyes full of fright, bloodshot, scared and shaking, tremors from the comedown. I wanted to protect him.

In treatment, I felt motherly toward the other patients. After a week of being in the house, I was the leader, having been appointed the "granny" by my house brothers and the staff. I ran schedules for everyone, printing them out in between therapy sessions; I sat front and center and took down as many notes as I could during lectures. In many ways, I became the same teacher's pet I used to be back in school. I was still overly willing to please, but it was genuine this time; I realized that I wanted to help others, not just myself. When Sam was still having withdrawal symptoms and couldn't stop vomiting, and the nurses wouldn't give him any more medication, there I went, dragging him to the nurse's station by his hand to try to help. I did this a lot. I loved every single one of my housemates like they were my real family. But I was still too afraid to fully share my real family story with them.

In my room one night, I sorted through the letters from my mom I'd brought with me. Some of them were addressed to all her children, and some were just to me. "Clinton, please guide your brother . . . we all know he's special," one of them read. The thought of her writing that brought tears to my eyes. "Colton, what a trip you are! You have done almost everything I strived for when I was young. Except being gay! Ha! I love your talent, but you know you'll need an education some day." That one made me laugh through my tears.

Another ended: "Colton, you little shit, I will come back and haunt you if you don't follow through on your dreams." I set it down and thought about it. What were my dreams? My dream had always been to be adored, to have endless sources of validation, to be seen—but I'd had all those things and it hadn't worked. What did I want now?

Sam knocked on my door. I looked up, feeling caught.

"How'd you manage to get your own room?" he asked.

"I had to pay double," I said. "I haven't been to rehab before, so I imagined I'd be rooming with a heroin addict who'd try to stab me with a needle while I slept." We both laughed.

There was a mess of letters around me, and all the photos tacked up on my wall, and my eyes were red from crying. He surveyed the scene. "Whoa," he said. "Miss Memory Lane, huh?"

I laughed. "Yeah," I said. "I guess. My memories are really all I have left."

He looked at the pictures: My mother as a young woman. Me as a little boy. This family of mine. It wasn't perfect. It wasn't the one I would have picked. But I was glad I had them.

He pointed to my mom. "Is she still around?"

I shook my head no, slowly.

"Sorry, man," he said.

"Thanks."

"I bet she'd be really proud of you," he said.

15

HOT SPRINGS, ARKANSAS
2018

A few months after Betty Ford, Meadow met me in Vancouver, where I had two more episodes of the show to shoot before that chapter of my life would come to a close. After that, we made our usual road trip down the Sea-to-Sky Highway, stopping at Porteau Cove, and traveled to the Scandinave Spa in Whistler. These were the things we'd always done together when she would visit me while I was working there, and they were places that felt like home, or at least the home we'd made.

We skipped rocks on the reflective water. It looked like a mirror to the sky.

"I'm sorry for everything I did while Mom was passing," I said.

"I can't relive that memory, Colt," Meadow said. She looked at the water. "But I'm sorry too. You know I love you."

After the wrap party, we flew together to Vermont to be with Julie, who was in hospice. She was wearing a small blue flannel shirt and she looked like a doll—a beautiful firecracker with locks of flame—but I remembered how she'd looked standing in front of the Eiffel Tower, and the memory made me smile. In front of her bed was the vision board with the skyline of Paris—I was happy to know it had been crossed off her bucket list. We applied cheetah-print press-on nails to each other's fingers. "I got to do everything on my list except visit you on set," she said. "But I'm glad I got to experience the real thing instead. I like you a lot more than your characters."

It all felt so confusing to me. I had only known Julie when she was sick. She was diagnosed with cancer even before I met her, and every year, we were all told it would be her last, but she stayed positive. Cancer had made its way into most of her organs, and even if she felt terrible, she wouldn't let you see it. The only difference in seeing Julie in hospice was that there was a hospital bed in their living room. She had looked rail thin and sick for years, but that's the only way I'd ever known her, which made it unbelievable that it was time for her to leave this life. She was still married to her high school sweetheart, Ken. The way he looked at her was unlike anything I had witnessed before—that love-at-first-sight expression never left his face when she was in the same room.

It hit me that Ken and their three kids were about to lose their life source—the same way I had lost mine. Julie didn't like to see me cry, so I saved my tears for when I went to bed.

From Vermont, Meadow and I flew to meet Summer in Arkansas. Clinton and Amanda met us there too. It was our first time being together since our queen had left her castle. It was nearly Christmas now, and I felt like I was a kid again, walking down Central Avenue in downtown Hot Springs, all of us bundled up in our cheesy holiday sweaters and funny hats.

There were enormous fir trees wrapped in twinkling lights on the road that led to the Arlington Hotel. I hadn't been back in years, and its steps were as grand as they were in my memory. From the lobby, I went down the spiral staircase, through the halls echoing with voices of visitors, rising in unison like a Christmas carol. I wondered if they had memories of this place like I did—if it was as special to them as it was to me.

In the old arcade, I pulled a quarter from the loose change jangling in my pocket. I wanted to feed it to the gumball machine, knowing I'd end up swallowing its contents like always, but instead I jiggled the handle the way my mom taught me, and out popped a gumball, like magic. I saved the quarter for something else. I knew I'd need it.

As we passed the fountain across the street, under the billowing plumes of steam from the hot spring, thicker than ever in the winter air, I stopped. My siblings were walking toward the car. "I'll catch up to you in a second," I said.

Alone, I looked at the weathered quarter. Its edges were worn. It looked tired. It had been used by so many. But it wasn't worthless. It had value.

I closed my eyes, took a deep breath, and tossed it into the fountain, making a wish that only my mom could hear.

16

PALM SPRINGS, CALIFORNIA
2021

First, there is a road, and this road takes me away from the house I'm renting with a friend for a month as I try to tell this story, all my photographs and journals and memories spread out on the kitchen counter, and a hopeful kind of sadness fills me up as I sail along Indian Canyon Road—the sadness of knowing that I have to go back to the real world on my own, and that means leaving some things behind, but I'm not ready yet.

At a traffic light, I pull over and get out of the car. I look up at the sky. There are windmills all over that part of the desert, looming across the horizon like unidentified flying objects. They're mysterious and welcoming at the same time: the way they spin, creating power and energy and light. The sun dips behind the mountain, making the sky a multicolored tapestry of pinks and blues and purples sprawling over the canyon. The wind picks up, blowing my hair back, and suddenly I am crying. I'm crying because for the first time I can remember, I'm present, and my emotions feel like a gift, a celebration, a reward. It's just me, myself, and the sky.

Now, driving on the freeway, heading west back toward my life in Los Angeles, I pass all the familiar places that stir up so many memories: the road that takes me to the hotel where I got married; the one that takes me to the rehab where I got sober; the church where we honored the life of my sweet Sam, my housemate in treatment, whose addiction got the best of him; the one that takes me to where my mom lived before she passed away—that one kicks up the most dust, and for a moment I remember what it was like to feel all that hurt and sorrow, and I feel like I am on a bender again, driving drunk through all the traffic lights, some green, some yellow, some red—a familiar game of stop-and-go, and then the sound of rattling sobriety chips hanging from my rearview mirror reminds me that I've been sober for years now. This road to sobriety—the only road I've ever been on where I've kept both hands firmly on the wheel, the only one I've ever taken slow, noticed the warning signs, and given pedestrians the right of way. I think about my brother Clinton, who is now one year sober, and smile.

Just past that exit, the GPS tells me to take another freeway, one I've never taken before, and for whatever reason, I do. On this unfamiliar route, I see things that remind me of my mom. The shuttered storefront of a Golden Corral, a restaurant I used to love as a little boy in Kansas, which I've never seen in California. A Miller plant, the same brand of beer she used to drink when she had an extra dollar to spare. Signs for the Huntington Library, which she used to frequent as a little girl, growing up in Southern California. A city I've never been to called Glendora, which she used to tell me stories about—she and her sister sneaking boys in and out of their window back when they were teenagers, breaking hearts and curfews. Back when life was just a one-lane road.

As I pass Griffith Park, I take an early exit. My shoulders are loose. The headache that was throbbing between my temples has subsided. I'm not crying anymore. I feel light and awake.

There's no traffic. I want to feel every streetlight washing over my blank canvas. She said she would haunt me if I ever gave up.

I will always be Miss Memory Lane. I promise not to forget.

I look to the sky and feel her ghost.

ACKNOWLEDGMENTS

First, there is a boy, a boy named Sam Lansky. Who isn't really a boy in age, he's in his thirties, but I'll always think of him the way I saw him in a photograph he showed me shortly after we met . . . wearing an adorable Mickey Mouse sweater and grinning so hard that his dimples almost crushed the frame of his polycarbonate lenses. Sam, this book wouldn't exist if it weren't for you. Your belief in my ability as a writer-storyteller is one of the main reasons I began to believe in myself again. After I'd spent years mourning the death of my confidence, you showed up and said "Nope. Not today sweetie!" and selflessly worked to help resurrect it. Thank you for your guidance, your memes, warding off raccoons and giant land crabs on our writing retreats together, and most importantly, for teaching me that one should never end a sentence with a preposition. Thank you for always cheering your friend on. Oops, my bad!

Peter Borland, it was a dream having you as my editor. Thank you for giving me this opportunity, I'm still in shock and incredibly grateful. Your prestige never got in the way of your patience. Not once did you censor me, or try and steer my writing toward a path that wasn't 100 percent authentic to the telling of my story. You treated me like an author and not like a washed-up celebrity. For that I will endlessly celebrate you, my friend. I look forward to answering the call when you ask me to start our next book together. I promise to try and meet my deadlines, lol.

Thank you to my book agents at UTA: Albert Lee and Meredith Miller, for working your asses off and being the best cheerleaders a person could ask for. Every time I tried to throw in the towel and flip the Gatorade cooler, your encouragement helped me get back in the game and cross the finish line . . . or kick the ball in the hoop . . . or whatever that sports reference is. Albert: I've printed out multiple texts from you and framed them to remind myself that my story is worth telling. Here's to many more group chats in the future.

Thank you to my film-television agents at UTA: Logan Eisenberg, Jonathon Weinstein, and my lawyers PJ Shapiro and Julian Zajfen for fighting for me.

Thank you to Alex Kovacs and Jason Weinberg, for helping to bring this opportunity to the table, and for convincing me to do it.

Ariele Fredman, my compassionate book publicist, thank you for noticing how difficult it is for me to read emails, and being so kind to correspond with me over text message. The time you've taken away from your adorable kiddo and fellow diy-ing husband to ensure that everything runs smoothly with the release of my book is something I hope I can repay you for in the future. Your daughter's drawing of me still sits beneath a perfectly placed ladybug magnet on my fridge. Thank you.

Raaga Rajagopala, Sean Delone, and Elisa Rivlin: Thank you for our marketing brainstorm sessions, for sending me early releases of books I'm dying to read, and for taking such good care of the manuscript. Oh, and also for putting up with my brain not understanding how to respond to emails. I'm starting to think this might be a theme . . .

Thank you to Marc Snetiker, Evan Ross Katz, and R. Kurt Osenlund for writing such beautiful articles that accompanied my coming out of the closet process.

Thank you to *New York* magazine and *Vulture*, especially Gazelle Emami, for giving me the space to write my essay

To my incredible family, my blood, my entire heart and soul . . . Clinton, Joshua, Julie, Summer, Willow, and Amanda. Thank you for continuing to love me, even when it isn't always the easiest thing to do. Thank you for constantly reaching out, knowing there's a 95 percent chance I won't respond. My love arrows don't shoot the way all of yours do, and at times it feels as if mine were stolen and replaced with knives. Thank you for going to war for me. For continuing to build the bridges, in order to cross the moat I've created around my heart as a preliminary line of defense. Thank you for protecting me.

Clinton, my bubba, my best friend. You are the person I look up to the most. Thank you for having a camcorder glued to your hand when we were kids, you captured some of my favorite memories, like the time you shot me in the ass with a BB gun and threatened to use the footage against me because I called you a stupid motherfucker . . . and the time I made you re-record my duet (that I did alone) of "One Sweet Day" by Mariah Carey and Boyz 2 Men because you didn't allow enough time in between my entrances . . . and the time we broke into that abandoned trailer and I chucked a brick at your face for scaring me. Thank you for dimming your light in order to make space for me to have moments in the sun. I'm sorry for being so selfish. Your willingness to spend your time after school, learning NSYNC choreography with me, is further proof that God must have spent a little more time on you.

Summer, my theatrical sister, the funniest person I have ever met. Thank you for not ruining my symmetrical face when I told you that the reason I seemed drunk all the time was only because I had shin splints. Your willingness to stay in your car for hours so I could read you parts of this book helped me continue to write it. Your altruistic approach to everything you do in life continues to inspire me.

Joshua: thank you for always holding me accountable, for calling me on my bullshit when I present an endless number of excuses, and thank you for being gay so I wasn't the only queer in our family village. Thank you for bringing all of us siblings back together again.

Julie: Thank you for showing me a love I never knew existed. I miss you every single day. I'll continue to search for you in every flash, in every flame. You are an eternal flame in my memory.

Amanda: you put your life on hold to take care of my mom in the end, when none of us could. Thank you from the bottom of my broken heart. You've dropped everything to help me get out of bed when my anxiety left me unable to move. Never stop "low dancing." You are my favorite (don't tell the others).

Meadow: thank you for taking me in and raising me when I had no place to go. I owe every success I've ever had to you.

You taught me how to be strong, independent, and how to fight for myself. Thank you for taking off work early and never missing one of my games or performances, thank you for creating a semblance of home for me so I never got lost in the woods.

Matt and Cassie: thank you for shaping my personality. You taught me that it's ok to be unique. Cassie: thank you for reminding me that none of us will ever amount to Amanda, I now know that to be true.

To my nieces and nephews, Jesse, Morgy, Taylee, Christian, Ellis, Wren, Megan, Emily, and Alex: thank you for not giving up on me. Thank you for calling me Uncle Coco, even after I continue to miss birthdays, and special occasions. When you're old enough to read this book, I hope you'll understand that I have a hard time expressing my feelings to the people I care about the most. I pray your parents have assured you that I really do care, they've also lived through it with me. Uncle Coco loves you.

Ally (or as your grandfather would call you, Ally Bally): my skeleton twin, my soul mate. Every time I write about you I start to cry. There really aren't enough words to describe how much I love you. Los Angeles didn't feel like home until I met you, and anytime I'm away from you for too long, I begin to feel feral again. Home is wherever you are. You'll have my heart forever. Trav: I love you too. Please protect our wife like your life depends on it.

Kevin, you are the "Valerie" to my "Mickey." The "Cristal" to my "Nomi." Thank you for the constant laughs, for keeping me stable when I couldn't physically walk, and for letting me capture you on video. We all know who the real star of Love Simon is.

Holland: You took me in when my addiction almost took me out. Ever since I was a little kid, I've always felt different, almost extraterrestrial. But from the moment I met you, I knew we were from the same planet. Please never stop talking my ear off. I love you.

Emily, you've never missed a birthday since the day I met you in Vancouver. You've never left a single ounce of space on any card or letter you've written me. You've maneuvered around every wall I've ever built, and gently held my hand to help me climb over it. Thank you.

Val, my dance partner for life: thank you for being by my bedside in the hospital, thank you for surrounding me with love and bringing so many genuine people into my life. The ways in which you help everyone will only continue to bring more incredible things your way. You deserve the world.

Sean: thank you for never losing faith in me, for traveling around the world with me to play Pokémon GO, and for driving hours to take my mom to the Casino every week.

Serena, Jill, Lex, and my fellow Kryptonians, thank you for not abandoning me after I had fallen . . . literally and figuratively.

Serena: thank you for all the ridiculous memories . . . that shady video from your wedding, tubing in Texas, dance rehearsal. Thank you for always pointing your toes, and remember that I'll always be an inch taller than you. Love you too, Lex.

Jill: the look on your face when I woke up in the hospital, we both knew no words needed to be said, and I heard you loud and clear. Thank you for walking around Beverly Hills with me when I was too sick to eat.

Thank you to all of my friends, new and old, for trying your best to keep me sane and for not turning your backs on me when I was at my lowest, I couldn't have made it through this book writing process without you: Nick, Ant, Nick M., Brandon and Matty, Ashlee, Alok, Rachel, Brandon F., Tommy, Kathy, Janina, David

R., Elise and Electra, Jack, Josh M., Travis V., Ryan C., Tyler H., Jimmie, Eliot, Ilana, Kelsie, Paul, Lucia, Kareem.

Trey: thank you for reminding me that I will always be Miss Memory Lane.

Thank you to the following for keeping me healthy, mentally, physically, and emotionally: Dr. Cohan, Dr. Richmond, Dr. Caplan, Tyra, Adele, Justin, JC, Joey, Chris, Lance, Jennie, Rosé, Jisoo, Lisa.

Thank you to my beautiful feline son Timothée ChalaMeow Haynes for putting up with my lack of sleep for the last few years. Daddy loves you.

Jeff: I'm sorry for the way things ended. Thank you for the most magical day of my life, it helped bring my family back together again, and gave us our final happy memory with my mom. I wish you nothing but happiness in the future. You deserve it.

Dad: It's taken me decades to realize that you weren't a terrible man. You were unaware of your trauma, and too stubborn to acknowledge it. I didn't understand it at the time but leaving that picture of me on your refrigerator, before you died, was your way of saying you loved me. I want you to know that I love you too, I don't blame you, and I forgive you.

Mom: This book is a love letter to you. Thank you for holding my hand every step of the way. I've made up my mind . . . forever you'll be mine. Oh, and one more thing. Thank you for granting my wish.